MAKING TOWNSCAPE

A CONTEXTUAL APPROACH TO BUILDING IN AN URBAN SETTING

Anthony Tugnutt and Mark Robertson

Mitchell · London

Typeset by Tameside Filmsetting Ltd
and printed in Great Britain by
The Bath Press, Bath

Published by The Mitchell Publishing Company Limited
4 Fitzhardinge Street, London W1H 0AH
A subsidiary of B. T. Batsford Limited

British Library Cataloguing in Publication Data
Tugnutt, Anthony
    Making townscape: a contextual approach
    to building in an urban setting.
    1. City planning   2. Architecture
    I. Title   II. Robertson, Mark
    711'.4   NA9031
    ISBN 0-7134-5315-X

TO BE BORROWED BY
ART DEGREE STUDENTS ONLY
APRIL - JUNE
1996

Contents

List of Illustrations

Introduction

If new buildings are once again to be compatible with their existing urban settings, we believe that there has to be a return to the tradition of townscape and architecture practised in Britain virtually up to the middle of this century.

Having visited numerous towns and cities throughout the country, it is all too apparent to us that the Modern Movement has caused a devastating rupture in the evolution of architecture in Britain and done irreparable damage to the hearts of many urban centres. We deliberately set out to visit a wide range of locations and this has provided us with a good sense of what has happened and what is currently happening on the ground.

Our reactions to what we have seen—massive and ugly town-centre redevelopment/pockets of historic buildings/lonely examples of sympathetic urban renewal—can but be described as violently mixed. Firstly, we have been truly appalled and feel genuine anger at the damage done, at the meagre, banal and tawdry urban environments resulting from the free hand given to architects and planners enthused by the Modernist credo.

Secondly, and more positively, we noticed how much still exists of real value that must be kept. This is particularly so in the north, where the Industrial Revolution has left an urban architectural heritage which lends a coherence, scale and sense of identity to the local communities.

Our final initial impression is that while there are some encouraging signs for the future, these are few and far between, and are more than outweighed by the mediocre or downright poor quality of so much contemporary urban building.

Essentially our concern is not primarily with conservation, important though this is in maintaining good and useful urban environments. Rather, we are convinced that a combination of strategies is required, of which building again from scratch is only one, though from our experience it is all too often the only option given serious consideration.

Perhaps this is an inevitable part of the regrettable legacy of the Modern Movement, with its philosophy of functionalism, coupled with an aversion to the past—whether of architectural or urban form—particularly the form of the street. This philosophy has resulted in several generations of architects and town planners being largely ignorant of, and lacking experience in, the use of an architectural vocabulary, once commonly understood and taken for granted.

The lay public has long been critical of post-war architecture and unlike its architects, abetted by town planners of the day, only too aware of its incompatibility with our older town centres. And yet all too few architects or schools of architecture appear to have a real awareness of the importance of a contextual approach to urban design. This is borne out by the continued design, illustration and criticism of buildings in isolation, with scant recognition of the relationship that new buildings should have with their surroundings.

A new approach

We believe there is now an urgent need to link together the growing awareness of the exciting possibilities of architectural expression with a more traditional approach to townscape, in order to create a satisfying relationship between new building and its context. At present there is a distinct danger that this new architectural liberalism will quickly degenerate into architectural quirkiness or mere fashion, remaining simply Modernism disguised in fancy dress; indeed there are disturbing signs that this has already happened.

But we are equally confident that this eventuality can be avoided if designers are prepared to study carefully the way in which opportunities and challenges have been seized in the past and used to good effect. And in studying the past, it is instructive to note the influence, whether conscious or not, that one design has had upon another.

To date, there has been surprisingly little published on this important aspect of urban and architectural design. Some notable authors have tended to analyse existing townscapes in order to identify those ingredients considered useful in creating new or replacement environments. For our part, we see the need to analyse the townscape to discover what a new building needs to do in order to measure up to its *existing* context.

We are aware that many, often conflicting, political, social and economic factors impinge upon our townscapes. If we have concentrated here upon the physical and visual aspects, it is certainly not because we necessarily believe these to be paramount. But we have come to realise that this area of interest has been badly overlooked and that there is an urgent need to redress the balance.

The purpose of this book

Our starting point in this book has been the general premise that small is beautiful; that evolutionary and pragmatic, rather than theoretical and radical solutions, are most likely to be successful, and, just as important, acceptable to the communities they directly affect. We have not, therefore, attempted to address larger-scale problems requiring the restructuring of whole quarters; these have been dealt with at length elsewhere. While we recognise that there may be good reasons for drastic changes and redevelopment to meet extreme situations, such proposals, especially when presented as easy answers or panaceas, should always be viewed with a healthy scepticism.

Scepticism indeed is perhaps one of the few positive legacies of the past thirty years. Most people are no longer willing to leave everything to the professionals—but it is salutary to reflect upon the cost at which this lesson has been learned.

Gordon Cullen, perhaps our best-known exponent of townscape in the post-war years, has suggested that 'one building standing alone in the countryside is experienced as a work of architecture, but bring half a dozen buildings together and an art other than architecture is made possible'.*

Although we agree with this broad statement, we have decided, for the purposes of this study, to restrict our scope to town and city centres, excluding suburban areas.

We have also consciously restricted our examples to Britain, believing it is important to write from our direct experience and working knowledge of British conditions and British planning legislation. This is not to say that as a nation we cannot learn from our neighbouring European countries, particularly in the way in which they use their streets and spaces to create a richer street life. But we felt that to include examples from the Continent would have weakened the message of what may still be found and emulated within our own country.

The structure chosen is intended to be a logical process of developing an approach to design, not necessarily reflecting the way it is usually carried out. The illustrations, mainly photographs, have been taken and selected with a conviction that a pictorial approach is an absolutely essential way in which to address this very visual subject. We have deliberately concentrated upon built examples, rather then producing our own theoretical futures illustrated by seduc-

tive sketches, as these have proved so misleading in the past. Photographs have the advantage of actuality and allow a minimal degree of misinterpretation.

Aims

In writing this book, therefore, we have had the following aims:

To explain and promote a 'contextualist approach' to the design of building in existing urban environments.

To provide a philosophical background and practical guidance to this approach, for use by students, surveyors, architects, planners and amenity groups. We also hope that developers and the so-called lay person will find themselves in sympathy with our approach.

To provide and support a framework for the current interest in an architectural tradition earlier than Modernism; and to demonstrate the importance and relevance of re-establishing a 'living building tradition'.

We hope thus to demonstrate, in practical terms, ways in which the lessons and traditions of the past can be understood and applied to our challenging contemporary situation.

Bloomsbury
May 1987

---

*Gordon Cullen, *The Concise Townscape*, Architectural Press 1971

Acknowledgements

The authors are pleased to acknowledge the services of Miss Peggy Wenzel for typing the MSS; Anthony Scott Ltd for processing and enlarging the photographs; the Controller of Her Majesty's Stationery Office for permission to reproduce extracts from Ordnance Survey Maps used for map nos. 3 and 4 on page 24; and to base map no. 4 on page 28 upon an Ordnance Survey map; Salisbury Public Library for the reproduction of extracts for maps 1 and 2 on page 24. The authors would like to thank Mrs Noel Heath for assistance in reading the proofs; the Cement and Concrete Association for their photograph for illustration no. 4.30; the Rolph Judd Group Practice for illustrations no. 5.149, 5.150 & 5.157; CGHP Architects for illustration no. 5.152; Kenzie Lovell Partnership for illustration no. 5.154; the Corporation of London Planning Department for illustration no. 5.156; the cities of Bradford, Sheffield and York; and Louis Hellman for the cartoon on the cover.
All other photographs were taken by the authors themselves on Kodak Plus X film.

The authors also wish to thank the many people who have given their time, advice and hospitality during the compilation of this book, particularly: Phil Baines, John Hare, Chris Curtiss, Jim and Ann Tyrrell, Mark and Isabelle Denyer, Fabian and Susan Robertson, Tim and Barbara Garstang, Yvonne Moir, Margaret Hollis, Robert Sherlock, John and Julia Tugnutt, the Community of the Holy Name at Malvern Link and Chester and, most of all, Robert Senecal and Liz Robertson for their unstinting support and encouragement over the past four and a half years.

Chapter 1

BREAKDOWN AND REVIVAL IN TOWNSCAPE TRADITIONS

THE SEEDS OF DECAY: THE VICTORIAN PERIOD

Georgian legacy

It was during the Victorian period that the seeds were sown that led to the eventual decay and virtual demise of our townscape traditions. The period had itself inherited the Georgian urban scene which, if at times a little dull, was certainly coherent, dignified and civilised. Many towns throughout Britain that prospered during the period had become almost solidly Georgian. Some acquired interlocking networks of squares and terraces while others had developed less formally, with individual Georgian style buildings along their existing streets [1.1].

At first the Georgian traditions shaded into the Early Victorian. Building styles looked much the same, residential areas continued to be built in the same form, and indeed even the main streets of the towns and cities themselves were largely residential. But the unprecedented expansion of towns with the Industrial Revolution brought change of all kinds. As their economies developed, towns had to absorb a whole range of new building types. In the 'public sector' there were new schools, public baths, libraries and museums, law courts, town halls, and churches. In what may be called the 'investment sector' there were new and bigger business premises, warehouses and shipping offices, banks and insurance companies, shops, theatres, music halls and public houses; all these new or expanding activities competed for space in and around the city centres [1.2].

Besides the building boom in the

1.1

1.2

1.3

1.4

1.5

1.7

centres and the industries surrounding them were the engineering enterprises of the Victorian period. The railways spread to link towns together, bringing with their prosperity the new scale of station buildings and marshalling yards, bridges and viaducts, new roads and parades of shops [1.3]. The Victorians were not particularly concerned with the art of formal town planning, rather concentrating their energies upon making 'improvements' to the often tortuous inherited street patterns that were becoming increasingly inadequate for the growing volumes of traffic. Wide straight roads were cut through and new circuses and squares formed at important junctions. Road building was also one way of solving the problem of slums. Other urban improvements were the very necessary measures of street paving and lighting, sewerage systems and a clean water supply.

This surge of activity radically altered the urban scene, at least in the towns reached by the railway. Taller new buildings invaded the domestic-scaled Georgian streets to create a new scale [1.4]. For the first time, town centres began to lose their residential element and become solidly commercial, and offices in various guises became the predominant building type. Architectural styles for these new buildings were at first mixed, being variations upon the Renaissance theme. But whether Palladian or Greek in persuasion, the well-mannered dialogue of their stone façades fitted well with the quiet but dwindling Georgian legacy.

Against this background, the Gothic Revival style was to have enormous impact. Fired by the impassioned writings of Pugin and Ruskin, the architects and builders who took up the cause were to despise the Georgian mode and to see their new building form not as just a style but as a whole system, linking back to a golden medieval age [1.5]. Their buildings therefore were in deliberate contrast to the previous classical-based era. Their arches, aedicules and polychromatic materials bore no relation to their older neighbours, nor were they intended to. The Gothic style indeed proved to be more than skin-deep. Architects no longer had to design buildings in which diverse activities were deployed behind symmetrical façades, as in the classical tradition. Buildings could adopt asymmetrical forms to suit their internal

1.6

1.8

requirements. Their construction too was versatile, and with the use of cast and wrought iron could achieve the large spans and weights imposed by the many new building uses to which it was applied. This new freedom of form and structure was to lead ultimately, together with other parallel threads, to the Modern Movement in architecture.

Exponents of the Gothic Revival were to clash with the Classicists in what may be called the first Battle of the Styles. These differences in archi-tectural belief were to introduce a new disunity into the street scene, Gothic contrasting with Classical, bringing a new emphasis on the individual build-ings [1.6]. Even so, in later chapters we are able to illustrate many instances where Victorian architects went to considerable lengths to relate their buildings to their neighbours.

Towards the end of the Victorian period another strong architectural movement—the Arts and Crafts—was to make a further and lasting impact upon our townscape. The 'Queen Anne' style of Norman Shaw broke upon the scene and introduced a second Battle of the Styles, which was to hasten the decline of the Gothic Revival movement, except for church building. Like the Gothic Revival in its own day, the Arts and Crafts move-ment was much more than a style, and under the influence of William Morris and others was concerned with a philosophy that included the building craftsman and a link with an earlier vernacular English building tradition.

Often beautiful, and always well built, Arts and Crafts buildings were immediately discernible by their fre-quent use of bright orange brick and contrasting white paint and stone [1.7]. The new style quickly became popular with architects and their clients. Like the Gothic style before it, being unfettered by Classical con-straints, it was easily adaptable to a variety of building uses and could be designed to respond well to their special requirements. Seen arrayed together such buildings, with their friendly, rather domestic appearance, with many thematic variations, make pleasing groups [1.8]. But one or two such buildings seen in isolation can introduce a very discordant note into the street scene.

Individuality

This individualistic style was to rein-force a tendency, already apparent in

Victorian buildings, to move away from a concept of cohesive townscape to one in which the appearance of each separate building was all-important, and the appearance of the street and the town itself far less so.

The nineteenth-century centres of some cities still remain sufficiently intact to demonstrate the Victorians' ability to construct fine, varied and interesting buildings, which yet create a homogeneous whole. There are other instances to demonstrate that the period could also produce buildings that were brash, egocentric and architecturally untutored. However, having endured a long period of misunderstanding and vilification, Victorian architecture is justly appreciated once more. When questions of saving Victorian buildings arise, it is important to consider the *group* in which they occur, for their group and townscape value may be as great or even greater than that of many of these buildings individually.

EARLIER TRADITIONS: ESTABLISHING THE RENAISSANCE

Georgian

The Victorian period had inherited a long tradition of deliberately ordered although by no means uniform urban appearance, reaching back to Tudor times and beyond. The Regency and Georgian periods that preceded it are sufficiently valued today so that what remains to us is usually protected by listing or within conservation areas. The noble sweeps of the circuses and crescents of our spa towns are justly famous. Many other towns, although their Georgian centres may have disappeared, still contain fine squares lined with elegant houses, some of which are sufficiently extensive to form sequences of urban spaces [1.9]. Almost every town contains some Georgian houses, often of individual design which, when grouped together, make a satisfying whole. Indeed Georgian and Early Victorian town houses are often more prevalent than is realised, if one can but discern them behind inappropriate shopfronts and unhappy alterations.

1.9

1.10

The displacement of many Georgian town centres by later development makes it more difficult now to visualise their appearance. Although in contrast to the Victorian town they were more domestic in character, they still contained the public and commercial buildings of the period: the town hall, law courts, corn exchange, theatre, assembly rooms and church; also inns, hotels, coffee houses and shops, all built (excepting those from an earlier period) in a unifying classical idiom. Smaller towns, not sufficiently prosperous to be rebuilt, had their Tudor house fronts 'Georgianised', or at least elegant new shop windows inserted on the ground floor.

Piazzas

But the tradition of planned spaces and elegant town buildings had been inherited from the Stuart, Jacobean, and even Tudor periods. Inigo Jones's Covent Garden Piazza of 1631 was to have a profound and lasting effect upon the British urban scene [1.10]. The Piazza introduced a new concept of shapes and appearance of buildings, were dictated to some extent by their construction in oak frame, brick or stone. Common characteristics were the gabled front façade and the mullioned window, the latter developing into one of the most beautiful features of a very 'home grown' building style.

Terraces

The earliest attempts to introduce Renaissance ideas into the country, combining them with Elizabethan, Tudor or even Gothic, were at first tentative, charming, and often a little naïve. In some districts the two styles became subtly blended, as for instance in the 'Tudor' brick buildings of East Anglia, and the Cotswold tradition on the limestone belt—a tradition that lingered far longer than elsewhere. By the late seventeenth and early eighteenth centuries, the Renaissance style began to replace the vernacular. In the towns, and even in villages, merchants were building their houses in the Palladian manner. Others adopted the slightly plainer and more anglicised 'Wren' version, usually in brick, in which only the shapes of the windows, the cornice (which also formed an eaves to the roof), and the doorcase displayed classical detail. These houses were usually free standing, or nearly so. Other town houses were built in the 'Queen Anne' mode: at first these were directly classical, displaying pilasters, entablature and a parapet, but they were eminently suited to fit into the narrower plot widths of established town streets and it was not long before the form was adapted to create whole terraces of houses. The terrace style was gradually simplified (partly as a result of the by-laws enacted after the Fire of London), so that in the plainest the only feature of individual houses to receive emphasis was the doorway and its surround. Nevertheless such houses could still be dignified, even beautiful. The secret of these attributes lay in the proportions of the remaining parts and in the fine craftsmanship of the brickwork of walls and window heads [1.12]. This type of house formed the basic unit of what was to become the eighteenth- and early nineteenth-

1.11

a square formed of individual houses, so grouped to make each side appear as a single palace. The idea of an urban residential square was quick to take root, and was to form the basis of development in London's West End from then until the end of the nineteenth century. The new concept soon spread throughout the British Isles, although the urban square without classical formalism had already appeared. Several of our towns, laid out in medieval times, contained rectangular shaped market squares.

And there was also the tradition of the more private type of square, as adopted for the quadrangles and courts of Oxford and Cambridge, and the cloisters and closes of the cathedrals.

The Tudor period itself had developed its own distinctive character. Being at that time particularly dependant upon local materials, this character was to have intensely regional variations [1.11]. 'Vernacular', in the sense of a style that had developed from the Gothic, rather than being imported from Europe, the

1.12

1.13

1.14

century Georgian terrace, manifested in countless streets and squares.

But the surge of Georgian building was concentrated in the more prosperous towns. Some lagged behind, retaining their Tudor character; others developed a mixture of Tudor and Georgian which can still be found today, and which has become one of the strands in the varied tradition of our urban scene.

LAST YEARS: 1900–1939

Variety and change in the urban scene, which had gathered momentum in the Victorian and Edwardian periods, continued apace through the 1920s and '30s. The profusion of architectural styles and new buildings makes late Victorian and Edwardian happy hunting grounds for the architectural historian. Perhaps the most impressive style of this period is that of the grand buildings of Edwardian Baroque, proudly asserting the sunset splendour

of the British Empire. Nevertheless the variety of styles, interesting and often graceful in themselves, tended to emphasise the move away from a sense of cohesive townscape towards the cult of individuality in building [1.13].

Rapid change

Stylistic developments alone, however, were not the only reason for change in the urban scene. The Victorian period had begun the drift away from town-centre living. In the

1850s shopkeepers and small traders had lived 'over the shop'; by the 1900s they were likely to live in the new suburbs, although in smaller towns the artisans might still be housed in narrow streets nearer in. Movement was to become more intense, and morning and evening migrations across town a normal feature. Traffic jams, already common in horse-drawn days, were compounded by the advent of the petrol engine. In the metropolis, the railway companies had completed a network of suburban lines, and these were to be augmented by the 'tube lines' and the electric tram. In the big cities, few walked to work and the centres became entirely devoted to commerce. The era of the office block had arrived, for shipping [1.14], banking and insurance in particular, which required ever increasing armies of clerks to staff their new premises. The introduction of the iron frame and the elevator enabled offices and commercial buildings to be constructed up to ten storeys high, where before four or five had been the most possible. The new urban scale began to outgrow its Victorian predecessor.

New building types

After the First World War, although office building continued, there were fewer grandiose examples, and the building industry concentrated especially upon the construction of the suburbs. In spite of the Depression, town centres began to display new building forms such as the cinema, coach and bus termini and the 'garage' or petrol filling station. None of these tended to fit comfortably into the urban scene, particularly the smaller-scale provincial towns. The bus stations needed large sheds and turning areas and the cinemas, besides wishing to appear very modern at the front, usually displayed huge asbestos roofs and blank walls at the rear and sides. Public amenity buildings appeared on the scene, forcing changes to many a traditional town, such as the General Post Office (with its sorting office and van park at the back), telephone exchanges, labour exchanges, public swimming baths and public libraries. Without planning controls, backstreet

industries could flourish and factories be started up or expanded where they had begun, with the result that many a 'historic' town became riddled with manufacture in the yards and alleys behind its picturesque street fronts.

The 1920s and '30s were also the period of the arrival of the multiple shop or 'chainstore'. The Co-operative movement, started a little earlier, was spreading with stores opening in most towns, and these were soon joined by Sainsbury, Woolworth, Marks and Spencer and many others. Most required large, generally new premises in their own house style, further eroding

the individuality of each town they reached.

All these new building types, together with the 'multiples' coming into town and into the high street itself, changed the scene still further. Some architects valiantly attempted to relate their buildings to the general scene, in particular in the GPOs of that period; others adopted a rather dull Neo-Georgian style. One contribution to debate on these new problems was Trystan Edwards's book *Good and Bad Manners in Architecture*, published in 1924. Other architects acting for the newer enterprises and wishing to

1.15

reflect the new age of speed, radio and aeroplanes gleefully accepted its counterpart of Art Deco [1.15], as may be seen on many an Odeon cinema where these survive. The cult of the individual building had arrived.

Many well-known architects' offices were to grapple with the conflicts arising between their classical or Beaux Arts traditions and the radical influences coming from Europe. A few were wholeheartedly embracing the writings and works of Le Corbusier and the Bauhaus and designing, not without resistance, what were popularly known as 'ferro-concrete' buildings. A third Battle of the Styles had begun. Their numbers were quite small, but numerous imitators copied their stylistic mannerisms such as flat roofs, horizontal glazing bars and 'streamlining', without much understanding of their underlying design philosophy. But the seeds of Modern Architecture had been sown and were germinating in the minds of the younger architects, to come to fruition in the post-war years.

Some of our smaller towns were less affected by these changes and by new buildings, carrying their peaceful traditional forms on for a few more decades. These were the market towns untouched by industrialism, serving relatively small populations. Bigger towns too could be less damaged by the influx, where buildings were large enough to be converted rather than rebuilt; or the towns were simply large enough in themselves to show some resilience in the face of rapid change. But in general it can be claimed that all these changes and innovations tended not only to alter, but to disintegrate the urban scene still further, without introducing anything worthwhile to replace what was being lost.

ECLIPSE AND REVIVAL: 1939–1980

Besides the Blitz and the effects of wartime social upheavals, the 1939–1945 war had other profound impacts upon English townscape. During the war itself, programmes were being formulated to tackle the problems of the old country. New measures were needed to eradicate slums, build better houses, schools, hospitals and roads, to clean up industry or to relocate it. For these ambitions, a change in the political scene and the extension of Town and Country planning legislation, combined with the objectives of the Modern Movement in architecture, offered a new and exciting vehicle. The tenets of the Modern Movement—daylight, sunlight and fresh air, better use of space inside and outside buildings and the embracing of new technology, all for the benefit of the population at large—offered ways of achieving a better Britain. Electricity would eliminate the smoky atmosphere, reinforced concrete provide new roads and bridges, light steel structures and the economies of mass production and prefabrication reduce construction costs, all 'for the benefit of the people.'

1947 Town and Country Planning Act

And so with the aid of the 1947 Town and Country Planning Act, the post-war rebuilding programme got under way. But as well as benefits, some of the doctrines, largely imported from Europe, also brought more disruptive elements [1.16]. Town planning was seen in terms of segregation and urban renewal, rather than of gentle surgery and repair. There seemed nothing to be gained from respecting older buildings in our towns, because they would not be there for much longer anyway. And besides, it was believed, if new and old did have to co-exist, had it not always been the tradition in this country that each age had built exactly as it saw fit, regardless of whatever else was already in place?

So it was that, slowly at first, but with increasing rapidity, our towns began to suffer a second Blitz. Under the planning acts, permission was required to erect a new building, but not to knock down an old one (although the listing procedure was by then in force). And planning consents were more concerned with land use considerations than with the appearance of buildings. A new and numerically larger student generation was passing out of the architectural schools, in time to help implement the post-war building boom, their training now firmly grounded in the Modern Movement. Functionally planned buildings, designed with a simple construction free from the influence of previous styles, may have been ideal for factories and schools away from other buildings on green field sites; but when the same principles were applied

1.16

1.18

1.17

to our high streets, the results were disastrous. The new, simpler buildings, unfettered by tradition or constraint, looked alien and temporary amongst their more sophisticated neighbours, their details unsympathetic and their materials tawdry [1.17]; and any savings made in this approach accrued (at least in commercial buildings) to the developer, rather than to the 'people'.

Thus the big new stores came into town, tearing down and building anew, or gutting and joining together unfortunate Georgian town houses to make bigger shop premises. Further down the scale, smaller shops replaced their Victorian shop windows with the biggest possible sheets of plate glass and hid the rest of their buildings behind brash fascia boards.

Post-war building boom

Still more was to come. To cater for growing public mobility and spending power, the concepts of the supermarket and the shopping centre were imported from America. To secure the large-scale acquisitions of land and properties involved, development companies formed liaisons with Town Councils. Planners looked for 'soft' areas of older properties suitable for this treatment. Many towns lost large parts of their historic centres during the '60s and '70s to make way for these new developments. Other parts of towns were lost to accommodate the motor vehicle—the rising tide of cars and delivery trucks, and the problem of through traffic. By-passes and ring-roads, requiring dual carriageway widths and large roundabout intersections, were carved out, creating swathes of destruction to keep the vehicle in motion. Still more land was required for the vehicle at rest, by way of service areas, multi-storey and surface car parks. Towns began to change, the familiar disappeared, finding one's way around became confusing, unexplained vacant sites and gaps abounded, destroying the old and very necessary sense of enclosure. The disintegrating scene was made worse by architects following the American trend of erecting freestanding buildings, surrounded by space, rather than enclosing it [1.18]. Meanwhile the general public, as yet insufficiently organised, grew increasingly alarmed

1.19

1.20

and frustrated at the speed of change, and at their powerlessness to curb its excesses.

Public reaction

Into this sad scene of destruction and despair entered some who began publicising their concern for the urban environment [1.19]. Ian Nairn wrote outspoken articles on the destruction of our towns, and he and others were involved in the famous issues of the *Architectural Review* entitled 'Outrage' and 'Counter Attack'. The same magazine aroused a new interest in townscape with the writings and beguiling sketches of Gordon Cullen. Frederick Gibberd published his *Town Design* in 1953. John Betjeman inspired a national appreciation of Victorian architecture and of leafy suburbia. The Civic Trust, initiated by Duncan Sandys in 1957, quickly became a focus for publicising national conservation and environmental issues. It also

encouraged the formation of many local civic societies and supported them in their struggle to protect their own towns from unfettered destruction and redevelopment.

Partly through the influence of the Civic Trust, the Civic Amenities Act came into being in 1967, and for the first time the Conservation Area became the subject of special legislation. At first the main objectives were to *dis*courage demolition and to *en*courage sympathetic renewal when this was necessary. Later legislation actually prohibited *any* demolition within a conservation area without prior consent. And although conservation areas were only selected because they were the most interesting or nicest parts of a town, the idea of contexture, of building with a respect for what was already there, did begin to be recognised as applicable outside conservation areas as well. At the same time the conservation movement got under way, and other societies effec-

tively used the media to galvanise national concern for what was beginning to be called 'our heritage'. Gradually, after many uphill battles, the conservation of buildings by refurbishment or conversion began to be perceived as a viable alternative to redevelopment.

Some local authorities revived the appreciation of towns (and, they hoped, their trading too) by giving rundown shopping streets a face lift, following the Civic Trust's example at Magdalen Street, Norwich. Pedestrianisation schemes became popular as one way of making a reasonable environment for shoppers and strollers. Supermarkets, and shopping malls as pioneered at Coventry in the 1950s, began—at least sometimes—to be fitted more sympathetically into the existing urban fabric.

All these initiatives were creating a trend in the right direction, but their effectiveness was small in comparison with the continuing scale of redevelopment operations across the country as a whole, most of which were displaying scant regard for conservation or context. And as a whole architects remained faithful to the tenets of the Modern Movement, even though for that reason the profession was becoming increasingly unpopular with the general public [1.20].

THE SITUATION TODAY: A TOWNSCAPE REVIEW

'Outrage'

Thirty years ago Ian Nairn, in the *Architectural Review*'s 'Outrage' number, warned against the rising tide of mediocrity in our towns, and against the American-style application of technology and of land-take resulting in what he called 'Subtopia'. Nairn and his colleagues were prophetic: the extent of Subtopia three decades later can only be hinted at here, but the American influence is only too apparent in our shopping habits and our town centre buildings.

A tour of our cities and towns emphasises, as nothing else can, how widespread and how comprehensive are the changes that have been and still are taking place nationwide. Every town has had its share of demolitions,

insensitive rebuildings, massive office blocks, big stores and service areas, car parks and modern buildings in a score of styles, none of which relates to their neighbours or to each other. Some streets contain such a chaotic diversity of buildings that there seem no two sufficiently akin to give the street some meaning. Shopping centres and shopping malls abound; and the supermarkets, with their attendant car-stack/shopping trolley systems, are so standard that they are now setting up in the smallest of towns. Some are brash and overbearing, others adopt a low profile and attempt to fit in [1.21]. All have problems of sheer size in relation to their traditional smaller-scale neighbours. A recent and growing trend is for the supermarkets, having made big dents in the centre of many towns, to pull out again to peripheral sites, leaving their problems behind them. The primary coloured hypermarket sheds pose another problem: with no pretensions to townscape, and lavish tarmac areas, they inflict further damage upon our traditional small-scale urban scenes.

A review of the architectural, surveying, and building magazines and journals tells almost the same story: a massive programme of rebuilding and refurbishment is still taking place in

our town centres in spite of an international trade recession. The architectural papers, concentrating upon the more interesting projects, suggest a higher standard of design than can be found in the majority of cases. The advertising material probably redresses the balance. Schools, hospitals, factories, even offices may look well enough on their semi-rural sites; but there is seldom an appreciation of the demands of building in urban situations. New buildings appear crude and gauche beside their older neighbours. The fashion for placing 'neutral' all-glass, or even all-mirrored-glass façades next to classical ones is still with us; or if not, unyielding rectangularly gridded elevations are offered as the only alternative.

Townscape revival

But there are also encouraging signs. With some new buildings an attempt has been made to respect their location [1.22]; some of these are illustrated in later chapters. There are projects in which the best of the existing buildings have been saved and re-used. Sensitive schemes are, however, still very much in the minority.

Pedestrianised streets are now commonplace, and have varying degrees of

1.21

success. Sometimes such streets seem comfortable and as if they have always been there. In others, shops and buildings appear like stranded ships upon a beach of paving slabs. But pedestrianisation is popular, demonstrates some care and appreciation of a town, and recognises that the environment has physical as well as visual components.

Conservation is now an accepted part of the urban scene. The majority of local authorities have chosen and designated conservation areas and at least attempted to retain their 'familiar and cherished scene' over the years. Listed building legislation has also done much to preserve and engender respect for our 'buildings of architectural or historic interest', even though there have been some notable instances where their being listed has not ultimately saved them from destruction. Official recognition of the setting of a listed building has also contributed to an improvement in local townscape.

Architectural commentators are becoming more aware of context as an important aspect of architecture. The Civic Trust, too, has been demonstrating its own concern with context, as is shown by its more recent annual awards. When the Prince of Wales made his startling remarks about glass stumps and monstrous carbuncles, in relation to the Mansion House Square and National Gallery Extension proposals, he seems also to have been reflecting a growing public concern about the disdain shown by some exponents of Modern architecture for history and for context.

There is, in fact, an increasing interest in buildings and in the built environment in general, as witnessed by the recent surge of books, articles, exhibitions and television series on aspects of architecture, town and

1.22

suburb. The trend towards designing buildings with reference to their context is growing, and it carries promise for the arts both of architecture and townscape. There are now a number of

buildings up and down the country which have been well related to their context. Some to which the authors would like to draw particular attention, are illustrated in later chapters.

Chapter 2

THE CONTEXT

2.1

The previous chapter considered the breakdown in our urban traditions and the recent encouraging signs of a revival of interst in linking up again with them. One of the reasons suggested for this breakdown was the cult of individualism in building, which increasingly drew away from local tradition. British towns have developed their character as a product of their history: that is to say, their geographical location, their original purpose, and their subsequent activities and buildings have each contributed to their present appearance. There is currently a keen public awareness and response

to the character of our towns, as is evident from the profusion of illustrated guide books on sale everywhere. And this is also proof that town and countryside may still be experienced and enjoyed, in spite of the violent changes they have suffered in the twentieth century.

In earlier times towns and their buildings automatically followed local tradition and practices; today, powerful forces are at work to homogenise the country, making town and suburb the same, whatever their county or region. But this need not be so. Without being either reactionary or

impractically romantic, there is no reason why necessary change should not respect the established and individual character of towns and use this character as an inspiration in new development.

It is very noticeable that the illustrations of the guide books mentioned above, and of picture calendars also, are very selective, seldom including modern development. Is this not a challenge, that contemporary buildings *ought* to be included and take their natural place in the views of our cherished historic townscapes, as a proof that they are accepted and even applauded by publishers and public, and not only by architects and planners?

THE WIDER CONTEXT

The local context can only be properly understood if it is considered in relation to the wider context. The factors that have shaped the character of a town, such as its geographical setting, the reasons for its originating there, and its subsequent fortunes and activities, need to be recognised as also having influenced the character of its smaller districts.

As can be seen from the following pages, the information, maps and photographs that may be necessary to provide an idea of the wider context can quite easily be gathered without exhaustive research.

This section also serves to suggest some of the reasons underlying the location of towns, their relation to the topography, and their various activities [2.1]. This photograph of a city nestling amongst the sweeping moors illustrates that theme, and at the same time demonstrates that the individual character of towns and cities may be viewed and recognised from the outside as well as from within.

The town in its setting

One of the pleasures of travel is seeing towns in their natural geographical settings. Many towns still proclaim their original connection with particular locations, originally chosen for purposes of defence, trade or communication. In others, later commercial and suburban growth has

2.2

2.3

obscured the original terrain that once supported their early existence. Conserving visible evidence of this relationship assists in retaining the unique qualities of a town, qualities that can easily be eroded by the insensitive siting of larger-scaled twentieth-century buildings.

Equally important is the need to protect the comprehensible structure of a settlement, so that the simple outline of, say, a church and supporting buildings is preserved when new development is introduced [2.2]. This particular town has been fortunate in not having to absorb larger developments. In fact, there can be few hill towns manifesting a hilltop setting so distinctly. The water meadows in the foreground below the rocky outcrop accentuate the sense of its isolation, and the engulfing trees suggest an unhurried pace of rural life. No building vies with the two church towers dominating the skyline, or spoils the impression of a medieval town clustered around them.

Low-lying towns may be equally conspicuous, expressive of their location and vulnerable to unsympathetic development [2.3]. The distinctive location of this settlement is accentuated by its siting at the bend in the river. In this view, the church spire is

perfectly silhouetted against the gap between the hills beyond, and beautifully reflected in the tranquil water.

Towns situated below hills can also have a strong sense of belonging to their particular geographical location [2.4]. This spa resort originally grew along the terraces and gentle slopes at the foot of the commanding hills, deriving shelter from their proximity. Later suburbs have spread outwards over the flatter land, to be checked in places, as in this view, by the sacrosanct boundary of a 'common'. The commercial blocks in the foreground are so strongly assertive that their scale, scattered siting and alien form are dangerously close to concealing the lines of the original formation.

Big cities, by reason of their sheer size, are more likely to be seen in parts than all together at one time and in one view. Even so, their physical bond with the land may be clearly understood [2.5]. Here, a series of bridges eloquently declares the presence of the hidden river and the imperative need to cross over to reach the city centre. At the same time the historic outlines of church and castle, that have for centuries emphatically occupied the high ground at the city's core, are now challenged by a prominent office block.

Coastal locations can expose settle-

2.4

2.5

2.6

ments to long-distance views from sea and land [2.6]. This settlement, situated at the far side of the estuary, again takes shelter from its protective mountain. Its view is enhanced and is particularly pleasing because no building has interfered with this fundamental relationship, or competes for prominence amongst the others. In fact, the recent development at the water's edge has been carefully designed so that its form and roofscape, although different in detail, has nevertheless blended with the older houses of the town behind.

Historical growth and present function

An idea of the physical development of a town can be gained from comparing an up-to-date map of the area with others from earlier periods. The first three examples overleaf were taken from the Ordnance Survey one inch series, located in the Local History

Section of Salisbury Public Library; most public libraries offer similar facilities.

Particular points of interest relating to these maps are as follows:

Map 1

The medieval 'gridiron' street pattern of the town is still the dominant

MAP 1: from Ordnance Survey First Series Circa 1811

feature, and indeed additional development beyond those perimeters is still minimal. A tour of the streets today, however, will reveal considerable replacement of original houses with Georgian. Function: market town and cloth manufacture. (The railways have been superimposed on the plates of this map prepared in the early 1800s.)

Map 2

Although the population of the town has more than doubled since 1811, Victorian suburban development is limited to a small area on the NW fringe and to infilling the railway loop on the NE of the city. Function: cattle market; local market; shops.

Map 3

This map, issued soon after the Second World War, shows only two significant areas of growth since the close of the last century: one on the N, spreading towards Old Sarum, and one to the S in West Harnham. It is still a small compact country town. Function: cattle market; local market; light industry.

Map 4

A mere twenty years later, a sudden surge in population expansion is clearly reflected in new suburbs stretching out in all directions, particularly to the N and W, almost connecting the city with Wilton. Function: cattle market; local market; light industry; commerce.

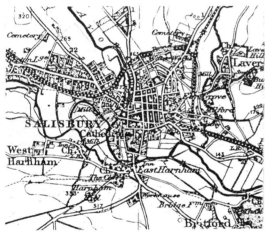

MAP 2: from Ordnance Survey series 1892

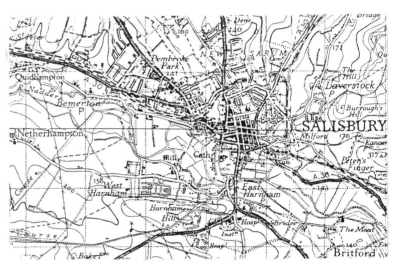

MAP 3: from Ordnance Survey 1″ series 1947

MAP 4: reduced from Ordnance Survey 1:50,000 First Series 1974

2.7

Main activities and dominant building types

In addition to the geographical factor, the individual character of towns will also have been shaped by their activities and the buildings related to them. Although this may be a truism, such an obvious connnection can be overlooked when old industries change or die. Many smaller industrial towns clearly display their main activity [2.7]. The brewery buildings appear to be the mainstay of this local economy and thus may claim a right to such prominence. The central structure terminates with a flourish, suggesting the pride of the company in its product.

Industrial buildings that have given towns their character are, even when vacated, still an asset both in themselves and collectively to the locality. They are often imaginatively designed, sturdily constructed and adaptable to new uses. They would also be very expensive to replace and offer far more potential when still standing than as vacant sites. There are therefore strong reasons for not demolishing redundant buildings before possibilities for re-use have been explored and their contribution to the local character evaluated [2.8]. The sheer numbers and size of these northern cotton mills create their own environment. Some of those in this view are vacant, and it appears that in this locality efforts are being made to re-use their magnificent structures.

When a new and foreign activity makes a large intrusion into a small-scaled neighbourhood, the result can be calamitous—especially if that intrusion is the only one of its kind [2.9]. There seems no valid reason why this office block should become the dominant feature in a refined Regency residential area. It is taking an unfair advantage of the sober location to advertise its presence.

If, on the other hand, office work is the main activity, there is a case for the fact being boldly stated with office towers [2.10]. And if it is to be towers, then gathering them firmly into groups is more appropriate. These office towers plainly proclaim their function and give a sense of identity to an otherwise sprawling built-up locality. The drawback in this instance is that the towers contrast starkly with the older, more domestic structures; and when the two are seen together at close quarters, the clash of scales is uncomfortable and extreme.

2.8

2.9

2.10

2.11

THE LOCAL CONTEXT

If any project is to achieve a high standard of townscape, it is vital that its local context is first thoroughly appreciated. Although the local context is often acknowledged to be important, in practice it is either consistently ignored or inadequately understood. This section is intended to suggest a methodical way in which to assess the local context of a project, and also as a reminder (and a necessarily fleeting appreciation), of the variety and quality of the townscape we have inherited. In any particular context, it is only by understanding and appreciating the value of what has been achieved there in the past, as well as its shortcomings, that we are likely to maintain or improve its character.

This illustration [2.11] has been chosen as a microcosm of the variety of local context: the street pattern converges upon a square.

Street patterns

In all towns except the deliberately planned, street patterns have not only grown but have changed and evolved over the years—a fact not usually discernible without background knowledge. A brief study of historical maps will reveal these changes, how they have come about and, in turn, altered the townscape. Developing an understanding of the subtleties of urban evolution will engender a greater sensitivity to change and can provide the inspiration for enhancement when opportunities arise.

The following four maps of a small section in the City of London have been drawn to illustrate changes that have gradually occurred since the seventeenth century.

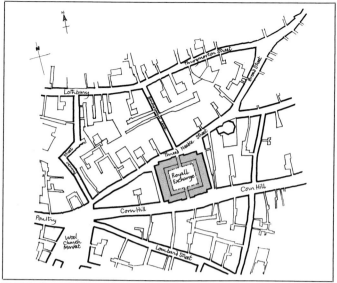

MAP 1: from Ogilby and Morgan 1676

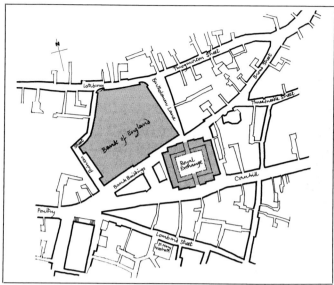

MAP 2: from Horwood's Plan 1792–9

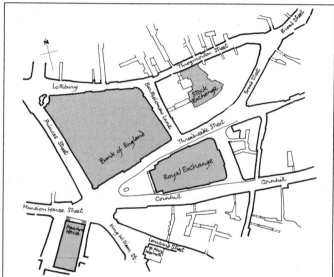

MAP 3: from Ordnance Survey 1875

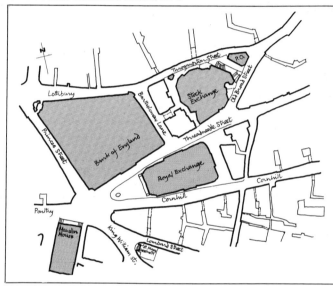

MAP 4: from Ordnance Survey 1983–6

Map 1

A largely medieval pattern of main thoroughfares radiates eastwards from their point of departure in Poultry. Between them lies a tightly-packed network of courts and alleys. Into these, the Royal Exchange (an earlier building than the one that stands there now) had its rectangular shape fitted awkwardly into a tapering site.

Map 2

The triangular strip of houses to the W of the Royal Exchange has been replaced, allowing a new connection between Cornhill and Bank Buildings to the N. The Mansion House has been built on the site of Wool Church Market. The huge perimeter of the Bank of England, resulting in the removal of many small properties, appears in the block between 'Threed Needle' (sic) and Lothbury; and its strictly rectangular SE corner results in Bartholomew Lane widening out towards its N end.

Map 3

The street pattern has again changed in consequence of new building. A new Royal Exchange has been designed to fit neatly between Cornhill and Threadneedle Street, and a new forecourt opened up to expose its most important side, the west façade. The junction of Cornhill and Lombard Street has been rounded off with a new corner building. The W front of St Mary Woolnoth Church has been exposed by the construction of King William Street; and with the cutting through of Princes Street to link with it, the pattern of the 'Bank Intersection', as it is known, has taken up almost the same alignments as exist today. Finally, the Bank of England has been extended to occupy the triangular site created by the new Princes Street; and the E side of Bartholomew Lane has been moved forward to take up the spare space caused by the realignment of the Bank of England site.

Map 4

In spite of the extensive amalgamation of sites in various redevelopments, the street pattern has altered little since the modifications shown on the map of 1875. The most significant rebuilding is that of the Stock Exchange, which considerably enlarges its site and, while not altering the street alignments, introduces new footways between Threadneedle Street and Throgmorton Street.

2.12

Spaces

Whether on public or private land, urban spaces form an important component of the urban fabric. Their functions vary from the main public square expressive of civic dignity and status, to the humblest quiet corner. Between these two extremes, spaces may be for relaxation, congregating, public meetings, shopping, markets, for residential areas or precinctual cathedral closes. They may also form part of a network for pedestrians quite separate from traffic routes.

In evaluating the local context, it is important to differentiate between the kinds of urban space to be encountered and the components that contribute to their character. This knowledge becomes vital when spaces have been altered or damaged after road improvement schemes or major redevelopment. There may be less scope today for the creation of new spaces, but when opportunities do occur it is of the utmost importance that they should produce the maximum benefit by being linked into the urban network.

Space is used as a compendium word for the various situations examined here; but whatever they are called, all spaces should be enjoyed and utilised for the enrichment of towns, by offering an alternative to the corridor street and a greater variety of spatial experience.

This internationally famous square [*2.12*] has been chosen to exemplify many of the aspects to be found in the study of spaces. For instance: the convergence of so many larger thoroughfares means that it becomes a natural focal point, but at the cost of bearing heavy traffic on all four sides; again, the wide gaps that these entrances create weaken the sense of enclosure; the unusually large size of the square demands a corespondingly large scale from the surrounding buildings which all do not achieve; the sloping ground across the square has been dealt with in a very positive manner; and the steps, furniture, fountains, sculptures and monuments have been well designed and carefully sited. Since the formation of the square in the 1820s, a number of famous artists and architects have, over the years, contributed towards its present appearance. These developments, and recent proposals for further change, emphasise that spaces are seldom static but instead tend to exist within a continuous process of evolution and change.

Formal spaces
Formal spaces usually present an impression of regular arrangement and a strong sense of enclosure. Equally strong supporting elements, such as the surrounding buildings, floorscape, furniture and planting, all assist to reinforce these impressions, and their variation will produce diverse results.

2.13

Large formal spaces
Low buildings in conjunction with proportionately large areas of floor-space, for example, produce a relaxed, more suburban environment [*2.13*]. In this most perfect of surviving Georgian squares, the symmetry is only gently defined by the central pediment over the houses on each side and by the landscaped oval garden. The high ratio of space to buildings, coupled with the plentiful tree growth, even in winter create an almost rural setting. Today, the beauty of the square is diminished by the tall office block beyond, which weakens the sense of enclosure. This is a classic example of the need to consider the likely effect of tall buildings on sites well beyond their own immediate locations.

Buildings which are proportionately high in relation to the enclosed space tend to be more formal and more urban in character. Spaces may also be arranged to interconnect, taking the place of the original street [*2.14*]. The foremost space in this sequence has been clearly defined and prevented from becoming a corridor by the

2.14

relatively small but very effective change in the alignment of the flanking pavilions in the middle distance, and the placement of the statues on their pedestals further define it. The formality is reinforced by the symmetrical facade which terminates the vista; and

the stately classical buildings place an unmistakable metropolitan stamp upon the whole design.

When some streets are pedestrianised their character is drastically altered and deprived of much of its former vitality. Others can be success-

fully transformed into outside rooms
[2.15]. The basic concept here has been
assisted by the church nave closing off
the end, reinforced by new paving
patterns and the geometric arrangement of trees and bollards. These
elements are sufficient to create a
recognisable formal space, in spite of
the variety of buildings on the right-
hand side and the asymmetry of the
church tower terminating the vista.

Another variant of the formal space
was the glass-vaulted shopping arcade
[2.16]. Although essentially linear in
character, in order to induce as many
people as possible to pass through, it
could be sub-divided into a sequence of
interconnecting spaces. Each space
formed an individual gallery with its
own character, in which people were
subtly encouraged to slow down again
and examine the window displays. This
example is a 'three-decker', in which
the height, in conjunction with a
beautifully traceried glazed roof, bestows a cathedral-like quality. At the
same time the dome over the end
denotes the intersection of this gallery
with other spaces left and right.

Small formal spaces
Besides possessing a regular shape and
sense of enclosure, formal spaces, even
when small, are usually uniform, even
symmetrical in composition. Such
spaces may be very small indeed and
still successfully convey a message of
composure and formality [2.17]. The
arresting appearance of this space is
provided by the happy proportions of
the classical façade, supported by the
matching but simpler elevations either
side. The steps, made necessary by the
imposed levels, further enhance the
formality by elevating the already
dignified principal building.

Formal space may be based upon a
variety of shapes [2.18], and in this
case, as in the previous example, has
been created with a modest use of land
by the simple device of widening a
narrow street. The small shopping
crescent is sufficient to provide a sense
of having arrived at a real 'place', and
its shape introduces a degree of
formality. Further definition between
the space and the street is achieved
with a flourish of stone staircases at
each end, while the arcade invites a

2.15

2.16

2.17

2.18

2.19

visit to the shops glimpsed between the columns.

Some spaces have been formed by the historical need for defence [2.19]. Throwing the battlemented gatehouse across the street has given a touch of protective drama to this once fortified hill town. The symmetrical design of the gatehouse introduces some formality and the central archway makes a compelling focal point.

The formality of spaces is sometimes reduced by planting [2.20]. In this instance the small square is so dominated by tree growth that in summer, at least, its regular shape is barely discernible beneath the foliage; although there is no doubt the tree gives it an air of distinction. The sense of the square's enclosure has recently been much enhanced by the construction of the archway with two storeys above it, in the right-hand corner.

Informal spaces

Informal spaces are as necessary to the urban scene as formal. Although more relaxed in feeling, they have often been deliberately planned in response to specific needs, and have developed their own individual characters for that reason. Nevertheless, some are certainly more 'successful' as spaces than others, and analysis is necessary to discover the reasons for this.

Large informal spaces

Historic urban spaces are particularly worthy of study [2.21]. This medieval space lies at the junction of three lanes outside a cathedral close gateway. Although large enough to contain the numbers of pilgrims likely to congregate at this point, the surrounding Tudor and Georgian houses are still sufficiently tall in relation to the space to provide a keen sense of place—visibly reinforced by the cross mounted on its elaborate column at the very centre.

In the design of informal spaces, as in any composition, the principal com-

2.20

2.21

2.22

2.23

landscaping is inappropriate, and finally, nothing has been done to contain the space or shield it from the intrusion of adjacent traffic.

Informal spaces occur almost anywhere, but do so especially at intersections [2.23]. In this case it appears that pedestrianisation has been introduced at a former crossroads. The danger was that the resulting space would appear too open and uncontained to be successful. But by the deployment of the refreshment pavilion, the haphazard grouping of railings and 'cycle racks, the bollards and, above all, mature trees, the area has become a natural and useful meeting place in its own right.

The churchyards and closes of churches and cathedrals are a valuable part of our heritage. As examples of townscape their quality varies considerably but many do in fact fulfil the expectations held for them [2.24]. In this example, the cathedral is the centrepiece of the composition and the surrounding elements complement rather than compete with it. The taller Victorian buildings on the town side to the left do tend to compete for attention, but are fortunately partially screened with trees; a small church and tower fills the corner, and the return side presents more humble houses of irregular heights. The broad areas of smooth grass keep all buildings at a respectful distance from the cathedral and lend it dignity. The total scene conveys an effect that is informal yet tranquil.

Small informal spaces

Small informal spaces spring from a wide variety of origins and needs, and in consequence their treatments also vary widely. Even the most simple and seemingly straightforward of spaces have involved skill in their composition. In some the force of the surrounding architecture has been allowed to dictate the spirit of the place [2.25]. Here, in what appears to have been a small churchyard, trees have been planted to contain the view, and the plain paving permits the classical wing of the church to speak without interruption from fussy flowerbeds and walls. The skill has lain in knowing when to let well alone.

ponents must be properly arranged [2.22]. This is an example of SLOAP, that is 'Space Left Over After Planning'.* The space in question appears to have been left over when a new

*SLOAP, a term coined by Leslie Ginsburg and to which the *Architectural Review* devoted a whole issue in October 1973.

inner distributor road was constructed; but an attempt to create a cultural centrepiece has resulted in an unhappy new space. The pre-war cinema and tower were originally designed to be seen at the top of a narrow street; the post-war theatre, screened with trees, hardly lives up to the role created for it; the soft

2.24

2.25

2.26

Courtyards, often privately owned, when arranged for sitting out and for shopping have advantages of protection from winds and traffic [2.26]. This recently opened courtyard has been planned with shops and a pub opening onto it. The planting, surrounding galleries, and well detailed entrance combine to create an attrac-

tive enclave off a busy street.

Even narrow shopping arcades have been forged into recognisable spaces [2.27]. In what might well have been an uninteresting corridor, a space has been shaped by the curved corners at each end, so that the shops are related to a specific location.

Road closures and pedestrianisation

are not automatic recipes for achieving successful spaces [2.28]. Here, in spite of the sculpture, there is little in the way of amenity to attract much use. There are no seats, the beam-and-post barriers are forbidding and the young trees seem unlikely ever to provide sufficient canopy to bind the space together.

2.27

Built scale

The built scale of a town is determined by the size of its buildings: their height, size of plot and average storey heights. Even where their styles and treatments are diverse, a consistency of scale can still be apparent. Some digression from the established scale must be accepted, but in each case there should be a recognisable reason for it.

Few towns are completely static and, by adapting to changing situations, they may gradually alter their size, status and built scale. But change made too extensively and too fast can bring a crisis of scale and produce disastrous townscape. There is a definable point beyond which new and larger-scaled buildings, together with their increased demands for servicing, overpower the original nucleus [2.29]. This illustration highlights the effect of massive redevelopment with an abrupt change of scale, isolating the remaining buildings without any possible means of integration.

Plot sizes

A common trend today is to amalgamate sites to form larger trading units. This can result in the rebuilding of new single premises which end up much larger than the average plot widths of a street, and bigger in scale. Sometimes quite bizarre contrasts can occur as if by accident [2.30]. These may be the result of thwarted site amalgamation for large developments when an owner refused to sell out, or because the site is occupied by a building of special architectural or historic interest. In this example the small eighteenth-century building will never be able to establish a dialogue with the scale of its brutish neighbours.

This raises the question: how large may new units be before their scale clashes with the existing buildings? There can be no simple answer, and the problem is intensified by the desire of traders to maximise their shop frontages. Where the character of towns and streets derives from groupings of small-scaled units, restraint will be necessary and will require less destructive, more imaginative solutions. Some types of operation—banks, building societies, supermarkets

2.28

2.29

in particular—need little window display area. Greater emphasis should be placed upon the quality of premises, instead of reliance upon mere size to bolster prestige. Expansion can sometimes be achieved by taking up disused backlands, or using vacant first floor accommodation, rather than by increasing the length of street frontage.

A frequent method of business expansion is for two neighbouring buildings to be brought into single ownership and 'knocked into one' [2.31]. This frequently occurs when the buildings are listed or in a conservation area and therefore must be retained, but it is desired to demonstrate that both buildings belong to the same business. In this instance the upper storeys have been left intact, the ground floors linked with a sturdy beam and column treatment. In spite of one being arcaded, this makes an unnaturally strong connection below two very different façades. There is also a very awkward point where the two share one column, which is not in proper alignment with their common party wall.

2.30

2.31

2.32

2.33

2.34

In certain situations, rebuilding may be a satisfactory answer to site amalgamation if carried out with sensitivity [2.32]. Here, not only have the earlier plot widths been reflected in the new development, but further variations have been made at ground level. The previous front alignments have also been faithfully adhered to. The third storey has been omitted on one unit. In these ways links have been established with other buildings further down the street and 'unified' development spanning four plots has been successfully integrated.

There are, however, limits to rebuilding within the small unit format [2.33]. The attempt is made here to lessen the impact of a major rebuild of several former plot widths, by suggesting their continued existence with varying facing materials. But by being recognisably linked at ground and roof levels, the development still reads as one building and tends to overwhelm an historic street.

Height and scale
The height of one building relative to another is an aspect of townscape closely associated with scale. The problem can become acute when much higher buildings are constructed on some sites, while existing ones are left behind [2.34]. The situation is not new however, as this picture shows. Victorian developers were not immune to

2.35

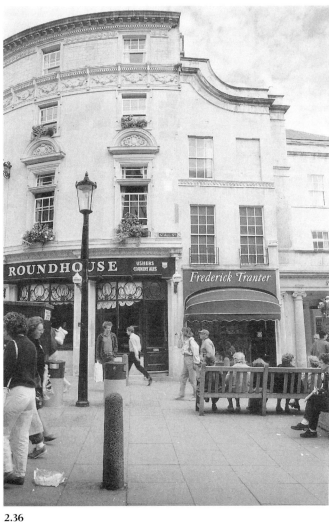

2.36

the temptation of building to bigger proportions and more effusively than their sober, domestically-scaled Georgian neighbours.

Scale is a question not only of size but of architectural treatment as well [2.35]. This classically fronted theatre increases its apparent scale by employing a giant order of pilasters and windows on its principal storey. The device actually overpowers the house on the right; and the same effect is apparent upon the recently built theatre extension on the left, which makes an insufficient adjunct to the powerful parent building. The theatre's scale and design were, however, sufficient to maintain its superiority against the arrival of the Victorian warehouse.

Ways can be found of relating higher buildings to lower ones when the discrepancy is not too extreme [2.36]. In this Regency example, the sweeping cornice of the narrow-fronted building

forms a successful transition between the disparate height and scale of its neighbours.

A combination of low storey heights, and too few of them, produces almost insoluble townscape problems [2.37]. An attempt has been made here, with the new block on the left, to lessen the disparity of height with its illustrious neighbour, by 'lining through' with the ground floor level and placing a pitched roof at the top. But its lack of height and the smallness of scale of the upper storeys in relation to those next door produce a 'doll's house' effect. the new block on the right has attempted to increase its apparent height but, viewed obliquely, is still insufficient to overcome its basic shortage of stature.

When the overall height of a new design matches those already in the street, the result is not automatically successful townscape [2.38]. The street façade of this embassy has been arranged to approximate the general

height of its neighbours; but seen in three dimensions, it appears considerably lower and lacks the necessary presence expected of its function. Its greater width and horizontal emphasis cuts across the established pattern of narrow plots. By this means the designer has made an unsuccessful attempt to fade the embassy into its surroundings, and to disguise the real bulk of the development; whereas, because of its function, it could well have been more prominent without being detrimental to the street scene.

BUILDING CHARACTER

The breakdown in urban traditions discussed in the previous chapter occurred not only in matters of architectural style but also in the sense of locality and of regional identity. When transport and travel were slower and more expensive, it was natural to

2.37

2.38

use local building materials and methods, thus creating local and regional traditions. From Victorian times onwards, easier carriage of materials has led to their being almost too readily available between one region and another. Improved travel and communications have allowed architects to practise on a national rather than a regional basis. Victorian and Edwardian builders fully exploited these new possibilities, but at the cost of eroding regional architectural character.

In spite of this, regional characteristics can remain strong. This section is intended to illustrate how, in spite of increasing neglect, local and regional character may still be appreciated almost anywhere in Britain, and to stress the importance of retaining such identities [2.39]. This picture has been chosen as typifying a strong regional tradition where, as in this case, the houses also display their own local characteristics. The other side of the

2.39

2.40

same coin is the British tradition of variety within individual townscapes. Our local styles and traditions lead not to rigid conformity but to wide variations within an overall harmony. The range of these variations is considered below.

Vernacular and local variations

Part of the richness of the British architectural heritage springs from these variations in character, between regions, between districts and even between different towns. Local building materials and methods have been a strong influence, on the one hand; on the other, local building styles, architects' designs and other importations from further afield have all played their part. Local building tradition has become known as *vernacular*—this term being generally used to include anything from the humblest construction in local style and mat-

erials to local interpretations of national or even international architectural styles. Many excellent books have been published on regional vernacular architecture, and the following is but a glimpse of the range of buildings to be found across the country. Many local building practices have died back during the post-war building boom, but there seems no reason why new developments should not once again respond to their traditional contexts.

Although the Georgian style is ubiquitous, local adaptations can be found, especially in coastal areas where balconies have added purpose [2.40]. These late Georgian terraced houses have iron projecting balconies incorporated with rarely seen recesses, above which a virtuoso display of gauged brick arches provide a distinct sea-side air.

Traditional Scottish building carries a strong regional character [2.41]. In

2.41

2.42

2.43

this recently restored example, the need for shelter is emphasised by large roofs and small windows, and shapes that are simple but dramatic. Care has been taken in the restoration to respect traditional details, such as the difference between the crowstepped gables and the peaked gables over their jettied bays.

The astringent appearance of black and white half-timbering is a common vernacular of some regions [2.42]. This type of structure has also generated other distinctive features, such as the jettying at each storey level and large gabled roofs. In this street the black and white houses are still sufficiently numerous to remain the dominant building type.

Flint walling is a strong feature of some areas, particularly where there are chalk beds [2.43]. Although corners and openings were often strengthened with brick quoins flint is in fact a sturdy structural material.

2.44

2.45

Materials and decoration

Materials, and combinations of different materials, have always provided great opportunities for decorating buildings. In the past, such practices have been very local in character. But in the post-war years in particular, although all kinds of material have been used many miles from their place of origin, their employment in decoration has been minimal. Such non-functional adornment of buildings, and the craftsmanship that goes with it, have been shunned as alien to the functionalist doctrines of Modern Architecture (and also, no doubt, because they would incur further expense).

At the close of the nineteenth century many buildings were very richly endowed with a variety of materials and their elaborate deployment in decoration [2.44]. Such a mixture of stone, faience, terracotta and brick, all assembled with heavy modelling, may seem unthinkable now; but the effects achieved, and their successful weathering over the past 90 to 100 years, are well worth noting.

This short section, however, is primarily intended to draw attention to the more humble and local use of materials up and down the country, and to ways in which their decorative potential has been exploited.

Even when local materials are crude and rough hewn, quite simple details can lift a building from the purely utilitarian [2.45]. Here the coarsely ashlared stonework has been carefully selected and laid around the window opening, achieving a satisfyingly strong appearance.

Hanging tiles have been popular in many areas [2.46], and have in particular been used to weatherproof timber-framed buildings. In this example they have been applied to practically every available surface.

Stucco was a popular facing material in the Regency and Victorian periods, and was considered a more superior finish than brick and as handsome as stone, but cheaper [2.47]. This example increases the dignity of a very small-scaled corner shop and house, with delicate panelling and decorative open balustrade above the cornice.

2.46

2.47

2.48

Unity

In some locations, and particularly in some streets, a unity between buildings exists which binds together the whole street. Variations have been played on the same theme, so that although no two buildings are identical, all conform to an underlying unity of expression [2.48]. In this famous street, the original units were allowed considerable freedom of expression within the overall classical formula. The unit in the centre of the second block displays a little more freedom in expression but still does not violate the underlying unity. Where it has departed from that formula, in its stepped attic roofline, the result has been to draw unwanted attention to itself. This has been exaggerated by the uncharacteristic angular mansard roof also being carried over the original corner building. Other Victorian work developed a looser relationship of styles, which nevertheless achieved a unity of a different order [2.49]. In this city street, Classical and Gothic Revival are set side by side. The turrets, cupolas, steep roofs, strong modelling, and the use of the same stone, provide a close relationship and positively link the components together into one coherent whole.

An underlying unity can also be present, even where a block has not been developed as a single terrace but as individual houses at different times [2.50]. In this series of Victorian houses, facing onto a market square, each one is individual in its height, width and details. Yet the underlying unity is emphasised by the slate roofs, prominent chimneys, strong eaves, stuccoed fronts and window openings, even though the casements within them vary. The post-war insertion in the centre dislocates this unity by introducing two quite different facing materials, strip windows and non-loadbearing spandrels, which have nothing in common with the traditional loadbearing walls of its neighbours.

2.49

2.50

Diversity

Exponents of the Modern Movement, to defend their right to total freedom of design, commonly employ the 'diversity' argument. Just as, it is alleged, buildings in the past were constructed according to the methods and style of their time with no regard for their neighbours, so today must buildings be designed and constructed in methods and styles appropriate to our own age, regardless of whatever may already

2.51

2.52

exist nearby. Furthermore, it is asserted, a 'good building' will always look well in any situation. In other words 'diversity', however extreme, is acceptable because it has historical precedent. But since the dis-harmony ensuing from this *laissez-faire* philosophy is everywhere to be seen, its defence deserves closer examination.

It could be claimed that diversity is part of British townscape vernacular. But successful townscape is a question of the limits to which diversity may be taken whilst still allowing harmony to be possible. If the diversity is too great, the result will be disharmony. An often encountered example of this is the juxtaposition between the Tudor and later periods [2.51]. In the clash between the staccato black and white style of the vernacular and that derived from more sophisticated Renaissance principles, the ensuing diversity is too extreme to be satisfactorily reconciled in any overall harmony.

For there to be a recognisable harmony, diversity must be contained within reasonable limits [2.52]. Although this group was not designed as a whole, an overall pattern is established by a combination of common elements such as plot widths, scale, the fact that its components were built for a common use, materials and fenestration pattern.

Group harmony is also possible when the elements are more diffuse [2.53]. In this typical market town

2.53

there are sufficient linkages of height, plot width and scale to help the group 'hang together', even though there are diverse elements such as style and material to create a much more free composition.

2.54

2.55

Uses

Some streets and districts have a distinctive air through being devoted to one particular use. The concentration of an activity in one locality has always been an urban feature and, as well as its being 'good for trade' that like businesses should cluster together, the practice adds another facet to the variety of town life.

Many streets display the time-honoured combination of shopping with residential—that is, shops with houses over [2.54]. Few streets so convincingly suggest, as does this one, that shops and dwellings, on both sides of the street, were constructed with this purpose in mind. The jettied overhang of the houses on the left add a sense of protection to the street, the small-paned shop windows invite the passers-by to stop and browse, and the bay windows above gently reinforce the domestic atmosphere.

Streets that were once residential but have given way to commerce are a common feature [2.55]. The centre building here has been rebuilt to continue the ex-domestic character of its neighbour on the right; in contrast the premises on the left are an unusual example of a purpose-built three storey Victorian shop, with display windows constructed at each level.

There are other streets where people

2.56

2.58

2.57

may still live over the shops latterly inserted on the ground floor [2.56]. Here, the recently built supermarket reflects this character, and it may well be that the upper floors are used for living accommodation.

A mixture of living and office use is another frequent combination [2.57]. The buildings on either side of this street could contain either flats or small offices, and the post-war infillings reflect the possibility of such a dual function. But the quiet scene is thrown off balance by the dominating, intrusive, yet anonymous tower block which overhangs it.

In some cities, whole districts have been developed for a particular purpose and in a particular form, as in this example [2.58]. The gridiron street plan and massive stone buildings with heavy cornices suggest a link with nineteenth-century America, and create a strong impression of collective grandeur. This conception is entirely overlooked by the post-war replacements, whose ambiguous glass curtain-walled façades devalue the intense identity and pride of a previous era.

Warehouses also generate their own unmistakable atmosphere of robust impregnability [2.59]. The new office blocks here have taken their cue from the original warehouse and thus retain the original character of the street.

2.64

2.65

VIEWS

Most of the town views in Britain are fortuitous rather than deliberately planned; but however they have come about, they are a precious asset. Grand vistas over long distances, and broad panoramas, need to be complemented by smaller framed views and informal glimpses, so as to achieve a richness of incident in the fabric of our towns.

When new developments are being considered, it is not always appreciated how they may feature in local views. Some research will be needed to reveal what the site and existing buildings contribute to the local scene and what opportunities there may be for enhancement. One valuable way of doing this is to take photographs of all available views, with which to form a proper record and a basis for photomontage studies.

Very few views in Britain enjoy statutory protection. Their continued existence, therefore, largely depends upon the vigilance of local communities and planning authorities, to guard against unnecessary mishaps and to seize opportunities when they occur. The view here [2.65] has been chosen to serve as a reminder that views occur in many situations: vistas and framed views down streets, glimpse views through gaps between buildings, and seasonal views like this one, which is a common occurrence in planted spaces, where a mini-panorama opens up in winter, to disappear again with the arrival of summer.

Vistas

Grand intimidating vistas are rare in Britain, having been only occasionally employed for royal or very formal locations [2.66]. In this unusual and imaginative example, the monuments upon their tree-girt hill create a strong contrast with the street below.

A more usual device is to site a church tower as the climax to a view [2.67]. In this case, it comes as a surprise, as the tower is not seen until the visitor has rounded the corner. The height of the tower seems excessive from this viewpoint, but it has also been designed as a landmark which,

2.66

because of its position on high ground, can be seen from long distances outside the town.

Vistas may equally be found in enclosed spaces [2.68]. Here the view culminates in a single object; and it is interesting to note that the opportunity to provide a focal point in the opposite direction has not been taken up.

Panoramas

Although panoramic views may be expected where there are hills and

valleys present, even when they are found they can still evoke a thrill of surprise and pleasure. By reproducing panoramas of breathtaking and unsullied beauty, guide books, and the tourist industry generally, have conditioned us to expect perfection on every occasion. Although this is, of course, far from being the general rule, there are plenty of lovely panoramas still to be found [2.69]. The height of this coastal town above the sea, for example, increases the distance of its outward views. Here the roofs of the

2.67

2.68

2.69

2.70

2.71

2.72

church tower on the horizon must once have been the only feature to punctuate the skyline. It now has unfortunate competition from the tower block which, with a far less memorable profile and modelling, can only detract from its simple dignity.

Framed views

Framed views may be discovered almost anywhere in any town. Some appear to have occurred by happy accident, while others have been deliberately introduced; but in either case they are a welcome addition.

It is not always realised that an ordinary street can form a framed view, so that what lies at the end of it, or beyond it, is extremely important [2.72]. Whether or not the tower of the town hall, which lies in the street beyond, was deliberately aligned with this minor street is uncertain; but there is no doubt that the church tower, the only visible building on that side, is sufficient to complete this perfectly framed view of it.

Indeed, streets need not be straight in order to frame a view [2.73]. The narrowness of this street first concentrates the eye upon the stone gate piers, and then its curve beckons one to explore what lies out of sight round the corner.

Archways perform the multiple role of framing a view and simultaneously enclosing a space on both sides [2.74]. This example is a reminder that the view through them is more successful when the eye is drawn towards particular subjects. Here, the Victorian monument has been carefully placed to coincide with the centre of the arch, as has the recently completed conference centre beyond, whose symmetrical front has been aligned upon the same axis. This being so, it is unfortunate that the symmetry has not been continued through into the roof structures, whose asymmetry presents a skyline that appears incomplete.

Colonnades are another and very effective method of framing views, at the same time forming partial screens [2.75]. In this unusual example, a way through has been constructed under a building, linking a street with a town square. The supporting columns have

houses on the lower level enhance the foreground, and the profile of the town beyond comes to a satisfactory halt at the cliff edge.

Other panoramas can be disappointing [2.70]. Here the abrupt contrast between the older part of the city and the twentieth-century development is very marked, but the opportunity to create an inspiring profile on such a prominent hill has sadly been missed.

It is heartening to find instances where efforts have been made to respect and enhance a panoramic view [2.71]. In this instance the open railings help in the appreciation of a view over the suburbs, from a central vantage point. The nearly completed roofs in the middle ground have been designed to relate to the traditional roofs further back, so as to produce a harmony in the general roofscape. The

been used to create a formal composition, through which the view of the town hall beyond is framed. Even from this side of the colonnade, the spectator is aware that the town square is properly contained, in spite of the wide opening connecting with it.

Glimpse views

Glimpse views can add enormously to the enjoyment of towns, especially for pedestrians, who have more opportunity to look around them. A planned town laid out on a grid pattern has few surprises and for this reason can soon become monotonous. Towns that have evolved more slowly have a greater depth of incident and detail.

Although glimpse views are usually thought of as having occurred by accident, there are historical examples to show that some, at least, have been deliberately planned [2.76]. Here the glimpse of an imposing medieval gatehouse was arranged facing directly down a lane, so that all visitors should know that they were nearing their destination.

Many glimpse views owe their existence to simple means of access; and common amongst these are passages and tunnels [2.77]. This example, leading from a busy street, is made more mysterious by its tunnelling through a medieval house and by the curve which prevents a view to the passage end. The time-worn cottages and stone flag paving also add flavour.

Other access routes can be entirely informal and provide quite arbitrary glimpses [2.78]. This pathway makes a short cut through a churchyard and its appearance suggests that it is of recent origin. It has drawn attention to a view which, although it has been there for a long time, probably went unnoticed until the pathway was installed. Fortunately this view enhances rather than detracts from the church's setting.

Some delightful glimpse views can result from a happy combination of chance fragments [2.79]. The unusual vaulted porchway can be seen resting upon its slender pillar half-way down the passage. The glimpse through the porch helps to make a second view, past the pillar, and out to the unexpected landscape beyond.

2.73

2.74

2.76

2.75

2.77

2.78

2.79

Chapter 3

THE SITE

In a contextual approach to development, the setting of a site, as considered in the previous chapter, must be followed by an examination of the nature of the site itself.

One of the failings of contemporary developments in our towns and cities is to ignore the townscape role of a site, the opportunities it presents, as well as the merit of its existing buildings. Multiple retail stores and national companies in particular commonly acquire large town centre sites by amalgamation. Many of these sites are then cleared of all existing buildings before being replaced by single monolithic structures, standard in design and visually inappropriate in their setting.

Good townscape can be achieved only by responding to the individual characteristics of the site itself: that is to say, its geographical position, its townscape role within a particular location, and the value of its fabric. This chapter suggests ways in which such features may be analysed and a site's potential for enhancement assessed.

TOPOGRAPHICAL

Geological

The relationship of a site to its geological setting is very often not fully appreciated, particularly the effect that relationship will have upon its townscape role. Hillside sites, for instance, not only present difficult problems of level for design and construction, but also result in the building itself, in conjunction with its neighbours, being more visible from longer distances. On

3.1

3.2

the other hand, sites located in valleys may be on level ground, but have particularly prominent roofscapes.

Hilltop sites

Obviously a town occupying the top of a hill will be conspicuous. It is not always realised that an individual hilltop site within a town, too, may be equally so. Far too often, the impact on hilltop sites of new developments is unforeseen and unfortunate [*3.1 and 3.2*].

The traditional British hilltop town achieved its successful and satisfying skyline from the relative uniformity of size, construction and materials of the smaller buildings, above which the larger institutions, such as castle, churches and town hall, rose to claim their greater importance. A hierarchy of size and shape eloquently expressed their individual and collective functions. The problem today is that new structures for more ordinary uses, such as offices and commercial buildings, tend to be larger than, and therefore to dominate, the older and still recognisable historic established forms. The situation can then be exacerbated by their rectangular 'shoe-box' shapes which are alien to the softer forms of their older neighbours, and are unrelieved by features such as bell turrets, cupolas and even the humble chimney, which the latter proudly displayed.

Hillside and sloping sites

A characteristic of buildings in these situations, as has already been suggested, is their propensity for being more clearly viewed from a distance than they can be from close to [*3.1*]—in some instances appearing in almost perfect elevational form. When, therefore, proposals are made for new structures higher and wider than their neighbours, they are likely to be particularly conspicuous.

This aspect of hillside development was well understood by Georgian and Victorian builders. It was particularly important when whole streets and terraces were contemplated [*3.3*]. Terraces, which are in essence long buildings, were designed to run either along the contours, or at right-angles to them. Both methods allowed economies in construction; they also,

3.3

3.4

through being in sympathy with the local topography and by making good use of the changing levels, showed off these fashionable ventures to their best advantage.

Larger-scale units can appear very prominent in hillside locations [*3.4*]. 'Getting the levels right' when designing for sloping ground can be notoriously difficult. A common solution today is to try to ignore the problem altogether. Thus servicing and parking facilities are situated partly below ground without undue excavation; and when these are combined with

large uninterrupted floor areas, the result can be very disruptive in an area of traditionally small-scale units.

Clifftop sites

A dramatic situation calls for a dramatic response. A site that can be seen from all around the coast, from out to sea, and from on shore, denoting the point where land and sea meet, can have no ordinary workaday solution. Buildings should respond to the scale of their site and to the rigours of the elements. Fortresses and lighthouses have an immediately recognisable

3.5

3.6

rapport with their surroundings for these reasons, an idea eagerly seized upon by Victorian builders with their romantic use of medieval styles. By contrast our contemporary coastal buildings appear flimsy and aesthetically unsatisfying. Bungalows are particularly inappropriate. Buildings of all types today, displaying vulnerable-looking low pitched roofs, sheet materials and an excessive deployment of white paint, appear to be, and probably are, extremely impermanent in such rugged situations.

Two major and successful responses to the clifftop site have been the eighteenth-century classical, and the nineteenth-century romantic. An essential element of the classical approach was to enclose and formalise space around the development [3.5]. Thus the influence of the building was extended over its surroundings, 'taming the wild' as it were, before allowing nature once again to assert herself at a respectful distance.

The later nineteenth-century informal approach took the opposite view [3.6]: the buildings were conceived in the romantic role as being *within* nature untamed. Rocky outcrops, clinging trees and frowning cliffs above a turbulent sea were a welcome setting on which to gain a foothold.

Level sites

Sites on level ground, not having natural features to enhance them, must depend upon the ingenuity of the designer to bring interest to the scene. When the numerous aspects of context and the townscape role of a site come to be analysed, the task may not be overly demanding.

There are some instances, however, where streets and even whole districts have been built on level ground in a rectilinear pattern and uniform building type, producing great monotony. Their corridor streets, between regular sides with no discernible incident, produce endless vistas from which eye and mind seek relief. Gower Street in London WC1 is often cited as an example of this, and there are several similar streets in West London. But Gower Street is only a small part of the Bedford Estate developed in the eighteenth and nineteenth centuries, and when the estate is considered as a whole it still provides a marvellous example of formally arranged townscape on level ground [3.7]. The straight lines of its uniform streets and buildings are complemented by the frequent interruption of the squares with their billowing plane trees.

This peaceful scene of uniform heights and domestic character is dramatically interrupted by the tower of Senate House [3.8]. Its great height and bulk has a legitimate role in announcing the presence of the University of London, which has now taken up a sizable proportion of the original estate. But dramatic interruptions must have good reason for their drama. In this instance the 'flagship' of the University has an obvious function and is therefore acceptable; whereas a block of flats erected to the same scale on that site would be an intrusion without sufficient reason for such prominence. In formal settings, generally speaking, deviations from the norm should respect the 'grain' of the locality, and any breaking away from it be justifiable and understandable.

Sites on level ground in less formal settings will have other criteria likely to

3.7

3.8

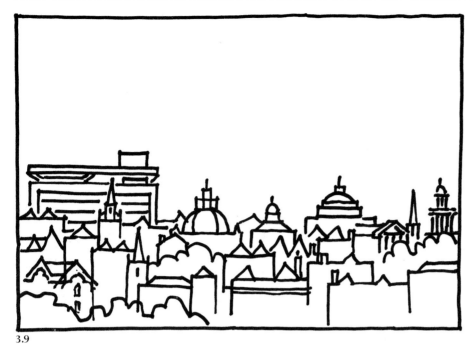

3.9

THE SITE
7.97 HA

3.10

bearing upon the future of our traditional inland waterfronts [3.10]. Large sites are opening up as earlier industrial buildings fall into disuse; for instance, local gasworks give way to North Sea Gas pipeline supplies, and railway sidings and marshalling yards become redundant. Much of this land, though often difficult to see, lies close to town centres. When such sites come onto the market, must they be taken over for DIY supersheds and surface car parking? Certainly such uses are necessary to the Western way of life but, as enterprising conservation projects have already proved, waterside sites contain local history, have charm and even solitude—exactly the right ambience for town dwellings created in converted mills and warehouses, for instance, or a mixture of uses such as workshops and studios.

There is obviously much scope to develop and make new use of these inherited but disappearing resources. Local authorities need to review their local plans regularly to keep abreast of events on waterside locations. Civic societies and amenity groups often have the vision to perceive opportunities for enhancing the amenities of their town, as well as the drive to make things happen.

Before sites are marketed and redevelopment proposals are submitted for planning approval, local authorities should have anticipated such events and developed detailed policies to cover not only such issues as land use, but also the infrastructure of access roads, riverside walks and towpaths, and landscaping, as well as policies on boating and fishing.

Development proposals for individual sites need first to consider issues such as why the site is for sale, whether any existing buildings are reusable, the nature of neighbouring buildings and whether they are likely to remain. Also affecting design will be the question of views from the opposite bank and from further away—landscaping, parking areas and security fencing are all highly visible components in such open situations.

As in the case of clifftop sites, developments on the banks of canals and rivers, being more closely related to natural elements, need a clear

guide their development [3.9]. For instance the relative heights of buildings will assume greater importance. And because sites are on level ground, that does not mean they cannot be seen from long distances. In fact the reverse is true: the roofscape and skyline of buildings on level ground can be as significant as in any other situation. Buildings taller than their neighbours are likely to have exceptionally prominent silhouettes.

Canal and riverside sites
A glance at a physical map of Britain reveals the large proportion of towns sited on rivers or connected by canals; some enjoy both facilities. But in many of these, their original *raison d'être*, of reliance upon the river or expansion due to canal transport, has become obscured. The decline of waterborne trade, sometimes to the point of extinction, and later industrialisation have gradually hidden our waterways behind factories and warehouses. A plea for a national return to water transport has no place here, but it is clear that the rapidly changing economic scene in Western Europe has a

decision on whether to be formal or informal in the design of the buildings and the organisation of the space around them. Waterside frontages will need to respond to the light-producing expanses of sky and water.

Geographical

Street sites

A typical-looking site in a town centre street of average width might appear so commonplace that its circumstances need but a cursory glance before designs for development can begin. Nothing could be further from the truth. Almost every site has its own unique set of characteristics. Aspects that will have to be resolved will include: the question of servicing, whether from the front or the rear; the need for vehicles to enter the site; the requirements of traffic authorities for set-backs or sight-lines; the width of the pavement, and whether offices or flats on upper levels require a separate entrance, with consequent loss of retail frontage.

Design of the building's appearance must also take into account its role in the street—the size and style of neighbouring buildings, and the fact that it may be seen from oblique as well as full frontal views and from adjoining streets [3.11]. The skyline may be visible from the street as well as from more distant views.

As the facts emerge, seemingly most unpromising sites begin to demonstrate their uniqueness, providing possibilities of individuality for the developer and design scope for the architect, to which both in their own ways aspire.

3.11

3.12

Lane sites

Lanes and their buildings are popular with the public and users for being more traffic-free, quieter, more intimate and more human. Generally, shop-keepers and others are willing to accept some inconvenience of vehicular access in exchange for the other benefits such a situation bestows.

In developments on lane sites, care has to be taken to respect the prevailing ethos [3.12]: great damage can be wrought by ungainly interlopers. Designs should acknowledge, for instance, that buildings cannot be seen as pure elevations (except perhaps from opposite windows) but only from strictly oblique angles. Conversely, window reveals, the modelling of façades or the slightest set-back or set-forward, is seen in exaggerated importance. Again, because of the narrowness of the street, shop fascias can be difficult to read, whereas projecting signs, if well organised, can add to the charm of the lane itself as well as to individual properties. The public are more likely to walk more slowly and browse along the shop displays. Shop-fronts can, therefore, be more appealing to the discerning shopper if the windows are smaller paned and if greater attention is paid to their finer detailing.

Lastly, there is also the possibility that lanes and minor streets may become pedestrianised. This can create a better environment for pedestrians, but cause problems of deliveries etc. for owners and users. But it can generally be said that, with reasonable co-operation by all parties, the difficulties can be minimised and the advantages enjoyed.

Sites on squares and urban spaces

An anomaly of the English language is the lack of an equivalent to the French word *place*, meaning a space in a town rather less formal than the English square. But whether in a formal square or a less formal *place* (both referred to as square hereafter for brevity), a building facing onto a square enjoys a privileged position. It is enhanced by being in a special location. Yet the square itself is more important than any individual building or any group of buildings that surround it. All three elements—individual buildings, their grouping, and the open space—come together to complete the whole, and the role of the building must be to complement and enhance the other two elements of the composition: in a word, harmonisation. Two examples may illustrate this principle.

Bedford Square in London is still a complete and beautiful square of Georgian houses [*3.13*]. To rebuild part of the square, if it became essential, in anything other than the original form, would be to spoil the original concept. Trafalgar Square, on the other hand, is flanked by buildings of different styles and sizes [*3.14*]. By reason of the sloping ground, the wide openings, and diversity of buildings, the whole composition is more diffuse. Leaving aside questions of conservation, any of the buildings could be rebuilt in a different manner without necessarily spoiling that composition. Furthermore, in rebuilding, it would be possible to improve upon the existing conformation. There is force in the opinion of some critics that the National Gallery is too low in height to be adequate for its imposing position on the high side of the square, and that being a national monument and institution provides it with another reason for possessing an enhanced stature which, at the present time, it lacks.

Harmonisation is the guiding principle in both these examples: in the first, emphasising the need for conformity; and in the second, highlighting the role demanded for a particular site.

3.13

3.14

Corner sites

Although so numerous as to be commonplace, corner sites offer great scope and challenge—opportunities largely ignored in post-war designs. These sites have social, commercial and townscape advantages over the others that lie between—witness the number of banks, hotels, pubs, churches, cinemas, fire and ambulance stations (and, alas, petrol stations) occupying corner sites. Consider some of their special characteristics [3.15]: they are more accessible, in practical terms; are more visible; and can, if so desired, become a landmark. In architectural terms they have a dual frontage; can be seen in three dimensions; and can be viewed from three or four directions. In townscape terms they may relate to five neighbouring buildings; have a more prominent skyline; and can terminate the street, and possibly the view as well.

3.15

Prominent sites

Historically, prominent sites were deliberately chosen: castles occupied strategic positions; cathedrals and churches needed to be central yet conspicuous; and the builders of town halls and markets often revised the street pattern to give them greater convenience and grandeur.

Today, hotels, pubs and places of worship still occupy some of the most prominent sites in town, but an endless variety of others continuously flow onto the property market. Some of these will have historic reasons for their extra prominence; others may be due to unexplained quirks of the street pattern, or to recent alterations from road realignments or demolitions. But whatever the reason for their appearance, they offer out-of-the-ordinary architectural and townscape opportunities not to be missed [3.16].

Like corner sites, prominent sites are likely to terminate roads and views, have more than one frontage and a potential for a striking skyline. In addition, they may be visible from even longer distances, be likely to be seen in silhouette and, because of their exposed position, be not merely a landmark, but a major 'town feature'.

Local planning authorities and civic societies can do much to encourage

3.16

appropriate buildings and uses on the prominent sites in their areas; and, by recognising early signs of decline and anticipating problems, local action can play a positive role in directing their future.

3.17

3.18

PLOT SIZE

Narrow sites

Very often a narrow site will be exactly the same plot width that has survived, with periodic rebuildings, since medieval times. Whole runs and groups of such narrow plots are still a common feature in many of our historic towns [3.17]. They have formed the backbone of the traditional shopping street, and been a basis for that charming combination of variety of style and local materials in our high streets for which Britain is justly famous. With a national tradition for such variety, there is plenty of scope when rebuilding takes place for expression and individuality in new building. But, as was discussed in the previous chapter, this is not to advocate a free-for-all approach, or to encourage, for instance, a steel and glass façade between two Georgian town houses.

The problem with buildings on narrow sites is their high proportion of service core to total floor area, tending to make them undesirable and uneconomic, leading to inevitable pressure for amalgamation. Where these buildings have survived, especially in urban areas, it is due to their pattern of ownership as much as to any desire from local authorities to retain their historic size.

Broad sites

When broad sites are redeveloped, they are likely to have more importance than neighbouring properties in the street. This may be satisfactory for public buildings, but for more ordinary uses, redevelopment on broad sites is likely to raise fundamental problems of size [3.18]. In addition to questions of scale and skyline considered in Chapter 2, the sheer bulk of the building is likely to distort the character of the street, unless from the inception of the design there is a determination to relate it to its neighbours. Equally fundamental will be entrances, and passenger set-down points and, in shopping areas, whether the street shopping frontage will be interrupted. There will be the question of whether to introduce setbacks into the façades.

3.19

Amalgamated sites

In practical terms, an amalgamated site usually results in an intensification of use, generating more people and greater demands for service areas and parking. It may well be impossible to satisfy these new requirements simply by using the main frontage: indeed the highway authority may not permit any intensification in that street. This therefore puts pressure upon land at the side or rear of the property. In small towns especially, the conversion of these areas for servicing, parking, and possibly storage, can create greater townscape and environmental problems than were at first anticipated [3.19]. For instance, walled back gardens will have to give way to extensive bleakly paved areas for parking and turning. The adverse impact will be felt well beyond the site boundary, with increased traffic in hitherto quiet areas, and large delivery vehicles plying along narrow back lanes, destroying pavements and bursting water mains!

Amalgamated sites often straddle lanes, short cuts and public rights of way; their curtailment, or bridging over, is a lost amenity to the area and to the whole town. Conversely, such sites may contain the opportunity to introduce a public right of way or some other facility or amenity for the benefit of the public at large.

EXISTING FABRIC: IN CONTEXT

Architectural quality and character

It is too often assumed that existing buildings on a site are useless and should be cleared to make way for a new development. Scant attention is paid to any architectural quality the structures may have; this is particularly true when they do not enjoy the statutory protection of being listed or within a conservation area.

But architectural merit can be an additional asset to be exploited. Tearing down familiar buildings to replace them with brand-new may be counterproductive, alienating the local citizens. Likewise, crude alterations to handsome buildings can have the same effect. But the careful treatment of old buildings, and sympathetic alterations, may assist a company's 'image', demonstrating that it has a human face.

This is of course, the conservationist view; but it is an undeniable fact that it is virtually impossible to find a contemporary building with the depth of interest, in terms of materials and craftsmanship, to be found in almost any building fifty or more years old.

Retention of older buildings should not be a slavish exercise in preservation for its own sake. Those with architectural quality in façades or structures should be adapted, and where replacements must be made

they should be carried out in harmony with those remaining.

Interiors

The interiors of existing buildings are often undervalued. Many contain interesting rooms, sometimes suites of rooms, and at the very least such features as staircases which, if retained, add enormously to their character. This can sometimes conflict with the contemporary desire for flexibility, meaning in practice uninterrupted open floorspace which can be subdivided at will. When the result is often a collection of small cells separated by indifferent partitioning under an uninteresting suspended ceiling, it may well be better to accept some of the original more characterful rooms, at the cost of a little inconvenience.

The banking halls of our Victorian high street banks have particularly suffered in this way. Equally shocking is the destruction of the ground floors of Georgian town houses for commercial purposes. There is no reason why, with a little ingenuity, the interiors could not have been adapted, and the essential stylistic and visual link between the inside and outside of these buildings retained.

Contribution to the local townscape

When assessing the merits of existing buildings, an aspect frequently overlooked is the relationship buildings have to their neighbours: the contribution they make to their particular group, and the contribution *that* group, in turn, makes to the wider setting.

A building may be poor in every respect, have no architectural merit, nor make a positive contribution to the local scene. But appearances can be deceptive; a run-down vacant building may look so parlous as to completely obscure its possibilities.

If, because of its instability, a building has to come down, its townscape merits should still be assessed. The best characteristics can then be included in the brief for its replacement and the poorer ones avoided, thus achieving higher townscape standards for the locality.

Relation to the wider setting

The local townscape to which the buildings on the site relate, relates in turn to the wider setting; thus the context for the site widens out concentrically to include the street, the locality, the district and the town. These buildings and the local group will be seen together in the same views; but visual memory will also relate them to the wider scene. There is often a recognisable underlying unity of built form in a town, of which architects and developers should be aware. Gaining such an awareness may require a little more time and effort, but this extra concern will bear fruit in a higher quality of townscape.

The wider context should be a concern of local authorities and amenity societies. Their familiarity with the locality can be valuable in assessing the merits and shortcomings of existing buildings in the areas where they live and work.

Group value

Buildings with group value are recognised, in guidelines issued by the government, as having special significance: see Department of the Environment Circular 8/87. This lays down that a building which is a member of a group can be refused consent for its demolition, if it is listed or in a conservation area.

Besides the obvious kind of groups that consist of uniform buildings there are those where the individual units are different but have underlying similarities; and there are groups that occur mainly by reason of their geographical arrangement. In either of these last two situations, there is a specific need to consider the site and its buildings in relation to the group as a whole, not only its immediate neighbours. In this way the site can be made to contribute to the local townscape, by taking the character of its group into account, and enhancing it where it is lacking.

EXISTING FABRIC: PHYSICAL CONDITION

Far more thought should be given to the possibility of re-using the existing structure than is generally the case. There is often a 'credibility gap' between what may be possible and what is thought to be possible. In some cases it may be that the structure, rather than the façade, is the valuable asset. For instance, the potential of the modern framed building for adaptation is particularly high, although this is not always realised. If the structure is re-used, the costs of demolition, excavation, new foundations and superstructure can all be saved, thus releasing a third or more of what would have been spent in totally rebuilding, for more advantageous spending elsewhere on enhancing the external appearance of the building.

Specialist advice

Appearances can be deceptive. The most alarming-looking defects can turn out to be easily remedied; conversely, severe structural faults are sometimes discovered only after a thorough investigation. It may be true that with modern technology almost anything can be repaired, but the application of high technology is usually expensive. Reliable specialist advice is therefore essential, and should be sought as early as possible.

Grants, loans and funds

The additional expense of renovating older property can sometimes be offset, if it is listed or within a conservation area, by Local Authority Grants. The local planning department will advise on details.

Grants for larger sums can also be made by the Department of the Environment and the Historic Buildings and Monuments Commission (English Heritage). But there is considerable competition for allocations from their annual 'global sums'. There are also many organisations and trusts which give grants for specialised categories of buildings, not necessarily listed or in conservation areas.

English Heritage, The Civic Trust,

The Architectural Heritage Fund and many others also operate loan schemes, on the revolving fund principle, for the repair of historic buildings. Procuring financial support from grants and loans is, however, becoming so complicated, especially when obtaining assistance from more than one source, that it is now almost essential to consult a professional who has proven experience in this field.

WORKED EXAMPLES

Introduction

In order to demonstrate some of the problems and possible solutions to be found in dealing with existing structures on amalgamated sites, two worked examples are given below. The first consists of four narrow frontages; the second has seven, plus a larger corner building.

The main purpose of both exercises is to suggest an approach which takes account of a developer's need to maximise a site's potential, but which at the same time also respects the existing townscape of a street and the role of the existing buildings on the site within that townscape setting.

3.20

Example: Site 1

The site chosen for this exercise has an imaginary boundary encompassing a group of existing buildings in a real street of a northern city.

The site
This fronts onto a secondary street which adjoins a primary shopping street. It consists of four separate commercial buildings each with an approximate 6 m (20 ft) wide frontage.

Assumed planning context
The area is for shopping/commercial use at a plot ratio of 4.5:1. None of the buildings is listed or within a conservation area.

Development brief
It is assumed that the site has been assembled over a number of years and is currently being offered on a 99 year lease for development as one or more units for office/commercial purposes.

Existing fabric
(i) *Description and townscape analysis*
Each building is Victorian or Edwardian [*3.20 and 3.21*] and is of individual and distinctive design, as are the other buildings in the street which remain largely intact from this period.

No. 1 has been much mutilated, but was originally designed to 'close the view' from the opposite adjoining street. [*3.22*]

3.21

Assumed planning context

It is assumed, for this example, that the area is zoned for offices/commercial, with shopping at ground level; the maximum plot ratio is of 4:1. The corner building (Building 'A') is listed Grade II but the site is not in a conservation area.

Development brief

It is assumed that all the properties are owned by one ground landlord who, now the original leases are falling in, is offering the whole site on a 99 year rebuilding lease, but would consider rebuilding leases for smaller units.

Existing fabric

(i) *Description and townscape analysis*

All the buildings on site are of the Victorian period: D, E and H date from about 1850; A was built in 1875 as a hotel, an excellent example of the restrained classical style in painted stucco, much used in the city during that period. The mixture of early Victorian/late Georgian domestic buildings, and their much taller, late nineteenth-century neighbours, makes for an interesting but rather chaotic townscape.

It is worth noting that the large corner building immediately adjoining the site on the left has lost its original pitched roof and chimneys. If at any time it was possible to restore these features, a far more adequate correlation would be achieved between that prominent corner and the substantial building A on the opposite corner.

As the aerial views show [3.25], the site is on the edge of larger scale developments, but not surrounded by them. Indeed the continuation of the same street shows a repetition of narrow-fronted Victorian buildings with a varied skyline, a feature of this locality.

There is a slight fall in levels from right to left along the site frontage.

(ii) *Structural condition*

For the purpose of this exercise, it is assumed that E and H have structural defects, including floors incapable of receiving office/commercial loadings, at least in their present condition [3.27].

Townscape objectives

A unified development could be appropriate here, but should be capable of subdivision into smaller units, both horizontally and vertically, as lettings demand. The rhythm of small frontages could therefore be retained to reflect this capability. The site should be re-organised to make full use of the servicing from the rear service road. Shop units should be based on the existing unit widths but capable of amalgamation. A pedestrian through-route, or possibly a shopping arcade, should be investigated to link through the block to the street and square on the other side.

Proposals

The main development objectives are as follows:

(a) To achieve larger and more efficient units of accommodation by some amalgamation of the present narrow sites

(b) In so doing, to allow for flexibility in letting by providing for subdivision

(c) To introduce a new shopping arcade, connecting the main frontage to the public square situated on the far side of the block

(d) To retain, as far as possible, the present character of the block and the contribution it makes to the street scene.

Details

The sloping ground and the total width of the site suggest subdivision into three, possibly self-contained, blocks, each with constant floor levels across the existing plot widths [3.29].

Block 1 consists of the corner building A in its entirety.

Block 2 is composed of buildings B, C, D and E with a new shopping arcade occupying the area of the former plots D and E. Buildings B and C are retained with the new structures linking in with their existing floor levels.

Block 3 is composed of buildings F, G and H, F only being retained. The existing floor levels of F can be aligned with those in block 2. Blocks 2 and 3 are therefore capable of being let independently or together.

New shopping arcade and pedestrian route

The demolition of D and E with their wider plot widths would provide the opportunity for a new arcade. To provide maximum flexibility, the floor level would align with the rest of block 2.

Summary

By dividing the site into two blocks and retaining the corner building in block A–C in its entirety (and one or two of the remainder), it is possible to re-organise and, if necessary, largely rebuild the site, without introducing radical alteration to the street scene. These proposals also allow a large degree of flexibility now or in the future. Finally, the new shopping arcade could inject new life into all the shops both in the block and surrounding it.

Standard speculative solution

Illustration 3.30 has been drawn in order to highlight the difference there can be, in townscape terms, between the contextualist and the 'clean sweep' approach to urban development.

3.28

Example Site 2

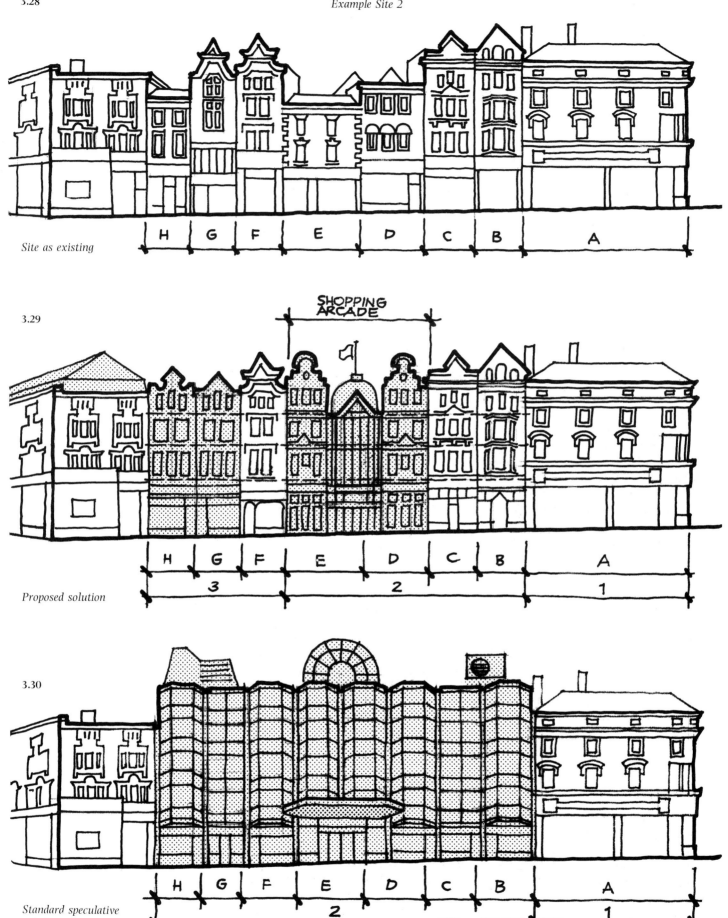

Site as existing

H G F E D C B A

3.29

SHOPPING ARCADE

H G F E D C B A

3 2 1

Proposed solution

3.30

H G F E D C B A

2 1

Standard speculative solution

Chapter 4

THE BRIEF

It is all too apparent that fundamentally objectionable developments are not necessarily the responsibility of untalented designers or a failure of the development control system. The inability of so many developments to address their context thoroughly can be traced directly to the brief. For example, an architect may be asked to achieve a far greater density than a site can acceptably take; however much skill and inventiveness are employed, an inappropriate scheme will almost inevitably result. Similarly, the client may wish to extinguish the existing mixture of uses, or introduce a new, more profitable use incompatible with the area. He may require that the design has a 'modern' or corporate image at odds with the context of the site.

The existing fabric on the site could well influence the final solution and the various options need to be given serious consideration. Clearly, when a site is in or adjacent to a conservation area, or is affected by listed buildings, this should be reflected in the brief. It is a question of modifying a client's requirements to the site, rather than vice versa. These aspects should be resolved before the site is acquired.

The brief should be tested at various stages in the initial design. It will be particularly important to make an assessment of the impact of any scheme on the surrounding area, preferably before a formal planning application is lodged. If this is undertaken, potential problems will have been identified and possible objections, by the planning authority or the local community, can be overcome and the

scope for conflict limited. Making the best of a bad brief is not a recipe for good townscape.

EXISTING FABRIC CHECKLIST

Nearly all our urban areas contain historic buildings and conservation areas. Their existence and the legislative protection now afforded them, together with public opinion concerned for their wellbeing, is having an increasingly important influence on the present and future form of our townscapes.

● Are any of the buildings presently on the site 'listed'?

Most buildings constructed before 1840 will now be included on the statutory list of buildings of 'special architectural or historic interest' compiled by the Secretary of State for the Environment. In addition, a significant number of later nineteenth-century and early twentieth-century buildings up to 1939 are also listed, and in future more recent buildings are also to be listed. All local planning authorities have lists of the statutorily listed buildings and other structures in their areas. These must be available for inspection. A list description tends to be written in a rather unfamiliar shorthand. It will usually include a brief mention of the salient architectural features of a building, and its grading. As the assessment has frequently been made solely from an external inspection, these descriptions often do not cover internal features; thus the omission of

something from the description does not imply that it is not of interest and unworthy of retention.

● Implications of listing

When a building is listed, this provides protection against demolition for everything within the curtilage, unless otherwise stated. Such items as garden walls, railings, outbuildings and even paving are encompassed by the listing. Any proposals to demolish all or part of a listed building, and internal or external alterations that affect its special interest will require listed building consent. This is in addition to any planning application which may be required. Control of demolition can extend to the removal of chimneys or other smaller features of interest; internally, this would cover panelling or decorative plasterwork. It should not be assumed that parts of the building not contemporary with the original fabric are of no interest and can be removed without consent.

When dealing with a listed building, it is advisable to consult the local authority. Many councils now employ specialist staff or utilise the services provided at county level. The Greater London Area has its own arrangement with English Heritage.

Although the existing structures on the site may not be listed themselves, they may be within the 'setting' of a listed building. This could be the adjacent property or one further down the street, or even more distant. There is a statutory requirement placed upon local authorities to protect the settings of the listed buildings in their area.

● Conservation areas

These are defined as, 'areas of special architectural or historic interest'. They are drawn up and designated by local authorities. The aim in these areas is to preserve and enhance their character and appearance. Plans showing the extent of conservation area designations in the locality will be available from the local planning department. Most authorities publish supplementary detailed guidance concerning both listed buildings and conservation areas.

● Implications of inclusion in a conservation area

The single most important result is that it gives the local authority control over the total or partial demolition of buildings within the area. Proposals affecting such an area will require a separate application, for consent to demolish an unlisted building within a conservation area. Such applications are judged on the relative individual or group contribution made by the building(s) concerned to the special architectural or historic interest of the area. So far as new developments are concerned, it is now established practice for there to be a generally stricter control over urban design matters, particularly in relation to their external appearance. But even when a site is not actually included within the boundary of an area, but lies just outside, it is still likely to be considered as affecting the area's character and thus subject to detailed scrutiny.

● Essential background information

In order to avoid abortive design work, it is crucial for the designer to carry out background research and the usual consultations at the earliest possible stage. It will be useful to investigate the recent planning history, not only of the site under consideration, but also of adjoining sites. This should provide an insight as to the authorities' approach to the area. The result of any recent appeals and comments made by the Secretary of State in his decision letter can provide helpful guidance, notwithstanding that each case is bound to be treated on its individual merits. On visiting the local planning department, the designer should ask all the relevant questions regarding any specific policies or requirements affecting the site. These are likely to cover density, uses, and servicing as well as urban design factors. Planning departments vary in their internal structure: different officials may cover the various aspects of development control, urban design and conservation. These local planners should be able to give firm and positive advice, making the requirements of the authority clear from the start. They are best able to do this if the planning committee has a consistent approach to its work, thus enabling officers to anticipate their reaction to developments. Clients and architects would much rather have firm guidance, even if they do not find it agreeable, than tentative or vague advice that is liable to change.

● Interested parties

Apart from the members of the local council there are other bodies who may have an interest in development applications.

The conservation area advisory committee

Many of these committees have been set up to advise planning committees on applications affecting conservation areas. Some of them may have wider terms of reference determined by the local authority concerned. They are usually serviced by the local council and comprise local architects and other relevant professionals, as well as representatives of local or national amenity societies and community associations. As their name implies, such committees are advisory and are not a substitute for the planning committee.

Local amenity groups

It is desirable to consult such groups at an early stage and, wherever possible, to involve them actively in the preparation of proposals, especially for major schemes. While this may appear to guarantee a time-consuming dialogue, it is a way in which objections can be overcome. These groups are likely to represent active grass roots opinion in the local community most affected and can exert a powerful influence on local councillors. It is unwise to attempt to ignore or bypass local opinion, or dismiss local groups as uninformed reactionary busy-bodies. In fact they often have access to expert advice from their professional members and possess an intimate knowledge of the area and its history. As such, they can be an invaluable source of information.

The Royal Fine Art Commission

Although seen by some as a rather remote, elitist body, this is taking an increasingly high profile. It has powers of 'calling in' applications it considers to be of public interest. It is open to designers or local authorities to seek advice by referring to it development proposals of a sufficiently major or sensitive nature. Although not having statutory teeth, the views of the commission can play an important role in any subsequent public enquiry. Where a local authority does not have access to the necessary expertise, the commission can form a useful sounding board, especially since its view in recent years has begun to reflect more mainstream opinion.

The planning case officer

When consulting the planning department, it is likely that the first officer to be seen will be the case officer dealing with the subsequent application, who will usually be at a fairly junior level in the hierarchy. Clients frequently press their architects to involve the chief officer, but this is not necessarily advantageous. To begin with, he/she is likely to have a full diary, but not be fully informed of the case history or of other discussions which may already be under way with other parties. Without this knowledge, which they cannot reasonably be expected to have, chief officers have been known to give encouraging informal views to a developer and then have to retract when later advised by their staff. It is important and in everyone's interest for the designer and planner to establish a good working relationship based on a degree of mutual trust. It is in such a climate that promising schemes are most likely to emerge and receive consent.

AVAILABLE DEVELOPMENT OPTIONS

Refurbishment and conversion

In most, if not all, of our towns and cities, the past centuries have left a rich legacy of historic townscapes. These are not confined to the famous set-pieces on the regular tourist itinerary, but also include more modest areas valued by the local community, although they may not be designated as conservation areas or include notable works of architecture. As Department of Environment circulars explain, 'they form part of the familiar and cherished local scene'. Wherever practicable, their refurbishment and conversion to suitable uses should be encouraged, since they provide an area with a sense of place and reflect its past in a very tangible way. Sadly, these structures are usually regarded as obstacles, rather than representing real opportunities, when occupying sites with development potential. All too often their true qualities remain hidden beneath layers of grime—their wealth of detail, craftsmanship and often vibrant colours obscured. When such buildings have been neglected they seem especially vulnerable, and their appearance suggests that their demise is only a matter of time.

Developers, architects and planners are only human. We all tend to assess things as they appear, rather than perceiving their latent possibilities [4.1 and 4.2]. These before and after illustrations demonstrate how, by simply cleaning an exterior, a transformation can be brought about. It is only to be regretted that this group of recently refurbished and converted buildings is adjacent, on the left, to one of the uglier examples of new public architecture in Central London.

Today, refurbishment can imply anything from rewiring or the installation of a new lift, to total gutting behind a retained façade. Limited refurbishment can be especially relevant to our older building stock in depressed areas, where funds are likely to be limited and where there will probably be a strong demand for low-cost accommodation. But whatever the extent of the changes, it will always be important to work with, rather than

4.1

against, the architectural nature of the building. This should ensure that thoughtless damage is not done to its character. The fenestration and window design are particularly vulnerable [4.3]. Here, a monumental and majestic warehouse has been adapted from its original use. By bricking up the central arched loading-bays and introducing an alien window pattern at the upper levels, its integrity and potential contribution to the visual amenity of the area have been seriously damaged.

Interesting internal features are often needlessly disregarded, usually in the name of modernisation, when, with a little care, their retention can add considerably to the quality of the interior. In cases where the client or his architect do not value such items, they must bear in mind that there are other individuals who do. Tight security can be essential during refurbishment, particularly to listed buildings; there have been many cases where fireplaces, panelling and even whole staircases have been unlawfully removed.

Conversion of buildings to new uses can help regenerate run-down inner

4.2

4.3

city areas and provide accommodation in central locations, at a lower rental than that for comparable space in new developments (although this will partly depend upon the standard of specification). By adopting this approach, the impact on the local community of the great economic and social changes under way at the present time can be softened, and familiar townscape adapted, rather than being swept away in a repeat performance of the disastrous '60s.

As noted above, when considering conversion works which include changing an existing use, particularly to office use, it will be crucial to check the local authority's planning policies on changing established uses. Developers generally want ground floors for office use, rather than for shops. Where this is permitted, the vitality of street life is diminished and the streets become a sort of wasteland. No one, apart, perhaps, from letting agents, is stimulated by ground-level office windows curtained with vertical louvre drapes, or prestigious marble-clad entrance halls, empty apart from a security guard, an obligatory set of Miesian chairs, and the occasional yucca plant! Few offices actually require to be located at street level. With such developments as automatic tellers, even banks may not need to occupy expensive street level space in the future. On conversion, 'the local' may be replaced by a basement wine bar [4.4]. An exception to the national trend, this successful courtyard conversion introduced a pub and restaurant with adjacent sitting-out area provided. The new multi-level metal access galleries have been sympathetically designed, to enhance the existing

4.4

character and create an attractive amenity to which the public have ready access.

Partial rebuilding

This strategy can facilitate the delicate surgery often required if the existing townscape character is to survive. Valued built features can be retained and, where possible, enhanced by other parts of the site being sympathetically redeveloped. The retained elements provide a reference point for any new work, while the designer is provided with scope for self-expression.

Churches frequently form important focal points in the general townscape [4.5]. There are increasing instances where redundant churches have been successfully converted for residential or other uses, while their overall external appearance has remained intact. But in this case, only the tower and spire were kept as a picturesque ruin, while the rest of the site was developed for expensive housing accommodation. It is difficult to resist drawing the conclusion that it would have been more satisfactory to have cleared the whole site to create a public garden for the use of the surrounding residential square rather than the present unholy union between God and Mammon.

Other buildings that have outlived their original use have been more successfully adapted to a new role [4.6]. This former bus garage, whose striking architectural treatment proclaims it as a public building, is now a local library. While it is not in any way typical of its surroundings, it does have the visual presence and distinction suited to its new use. The apparently separate brick infill on the left is part of a new extension to the retained terra cotta façade. Although it was absolutely right for the designer not to attempt to extend the three-bay façade in replica, the addition is perhaps a little too underplayed.

Partial rebuilding has the distinct advantage of assisting the retention of the existing built scale [4.7]. It avoids the often invidious situation resulting from total site clearance, where a designer may then be required, often by the local authority, to attempt to

4.5

4.6

break down artificially the apparent scale of a development by employing stylistic devices which strike an unconvincing note. The end result still reads as an over-large, unified development, in spite of the best endeavours of the architect. Here, while there may be reservations about the new extension, there is a clear distinction between it and the retained façade which helps reduce the impact of the unified spaces provided by the overall scheme. An additional benefit flowing from selective rebuilding is that it can greatly assist building operations by providing access to the site, as this can often cause considerable difficulties in densely developed urban areas. It can also be of great assistance when considering the retention of a group of buildings where floor levels or fenestration are at odds with the rest. Limited redevelopment here can assist in overcoming the difficulties otherwise likely to put the proposals in jeopardy.

Façade retention

This increasingly common practice, while rarely appropriate for historic buildings with interesting interiors or methods of construction, does mean that the façades of buildings of real townscape interest can be retained, and thus continue to make a contribution to their surroundings. Splendid façades representing unrepeatable craftsmanship can often be preserved to enrich and stimulate future generations. They provide a living sense of history which the built environment readily conveys.

The Victorians and Edwardians spent money on creating an imposing external effect—on the main street frontages—while the interiors can be surprisingly meagre. In practice, there can be little logical objection to this process, known somewhat disparagingly as 'façadism'; it is, in fact, very appropriate for the numerous buildings conceived as street frontages.

Of course there can be difficulties arising from this treatment; for example, if the site in question is land-locked, then the only access for site deliveries during building work has to be gained through existing openings in the retained wall. There is also the inevit-

4.7

able cost of the structural works to support the façade during rebuilding, and the obstruction that these can cause. On the positive side, the generous floor to ceiling heights of many nineteenth- and early twentieth-century buildings means that current and future servicing requirements, provided through suspended ceilings and raised floors, can usually be accommodated within the constraints imposed by the retained façade. This is in direct contrast to many developments dating from the 1950s and '60s.

It is always important to ensure that new floor levels relate as satisfactorily as possible to the existing window openings. It can be acceptable to introduce set-back bulkheads internally to overcome the slight inconsistencies bound to arise, particularly at upper levels.

There is no doubt that façade retention is unpopular with certain members of the architectural fraternity, as it denies them the opportunity to leave their mark on the townscape through the degree of modesty and self-

4.8

restraint required. But as younger architects once again explore the richer architectural vocabulary illustrated by our built heritage, there is a growing appreciation of the skill and ingenuity of many pre-Modern architects. It is to be hoped that, in future, architects may not be quite so willing, as they have been in the past quarter century, to relegate the considerable achievements of their predecessors to the 'dustbin' of history. The responsibility for this destructive attitude to the past can be laid directly at the door of the Modern Movement.

Usually, the principal justification for façadism is to preserve the character of a piece of townscape or the integrity of a group of buildings. When carrying out this exercise, it is crucial to treat the subject with due respect [4.8]. Perhaps, in this case, good intentions turned rapidly into a bad visual joke. Although this elegant classical façade was clearly worth saving in its own right, it requires an

appropriate setting in order to perform in the street scene, where it closes the view down the facing street. Now forming part of a supermarket complex, it has been denied a specific function. It could have formed an impressive entrance, which in fact is situated just out of sight to the left. Instead, the passer-by who is foolish enough to glance through the ground-floor windows is confronted by a boiler and gleaming pipework. It would appear that the designer intended to provide a 'neutral foil' to the retained façade, whereas he has, in fact, cast it adrift and reduced it to meaningless architectural stage scenery.

A significant number of buildings, still typical of the historic cores of most of our towns and cities, recall the past, not only by their overall design and distinctive character, but also by their quality and richness of detail. This is something that is difficult, if not impossible, to recapture [4.9]. Here, the reason for retention is partly intrinsic

architectural interest, and partly the relationship the retained façade forms with its neighbours. Sadly, it is difficult to imagine a new building providing an adequate replacement on either of these counts.

The difficulty of illustrating good examples of façade retention is that, when it is well done, the fact that only the frontage has been kept with a new building constructed behind should not be apparent [4.10]. As with this example, the nature of the architecture can help. The arcaded façade of the old market has been preserved with a new library provided to the rear. A prominent feature seen from the Market Square, this façade also forms an important part of an attractive group.

An approach to façade retention favoured by some designers is to keep the retained external wall as a distinct element, and to erect a new building behind it, unrelated to its architectural character. One practical reason for this is to permit the introduction of standar-

4.9

dised floor to ceiling heights. This can result in some levels having little, if any, natural light. It can also create an unhappy visual effect when viewed from outside. This detracts from the integrity of the façade and its continuing contribution to the townscape [*4.11*]. The monumental stonework of this 1920s building has been retained and large areas of a reflective high-tech glazing system have been provided, partly to obscure the floor levels. The designers concerned possibly argued that this solution allowed the classical detail to speak for itself. The new roof storey carried across to the new extension on the right strikes a discordant note, with each pier below reflected up the fully glazed mansard like a series of party walls. The overall impression of an assertive, reflective box trying to burst through its classical wrapping is disconcerting, to say the least. The end result hardly seems worth all the effort and expense involved.

Replica rebuild

This option is sometimes proposed as a palatable alternative to façade retention. Retaining façades, as has already been mentioned, can be an expensive enterprise, and new construction will nearly always be more attractive to conservative funding institutions. In addition, the vagaries of the tax system, and in particular Value Added Tax, can provide a significant inducement to demolish and build anew.

Architects, planning authorities and local amenity groups should be fully aware of the potential pitfalls. To begin with, it is often not practicable to rebuild façades—which are normally of a monolithic, load-bearing construction—and produce the same appearance as before, using present constructional methods and complying with current building regulations. It can be difficult to match materials

4.10

4.11

precisely, or corners may be cut by using artificial, rather than natural stone; windows are often subject to insensitive alterations. It is not unknown for designers to attempt to 'improve' on the original by subtly altering the proportions. While each deviation considered on its own may be reasonable, their cumulative effect can result in something far removed from the original.

Perhaps the most valid objection to this practice is the inevitable loss of authenticity—often a primary motivation for seeking the retention of a structure in the first place. While this may seem to be a nice point in relation to general townscape values, the way a building has weathered and been adapted and the fact that it looks its age are positive contributions to the townscape. On rebuilding, there is frequently a temptation to over-restore and thereby remove the minor changes that make an individual building unique. It is this rather purist attitude

that can make replica buildings appear unreal [4.12]. This represents a laudable attempt to help the recreation of a much-altered square; but in spite of the obvious careful attention to detail, the recently constructed series of buildings does not look terribly convincing, even from a distance. All the windows have a standardised pattern of subdivision. Party walls, which emphasise the underlying scale, have not been adequately expressed, and this, combined with a lack of chimney stacks and resulting simplified roofline, creates a somewhat artificial atmosphere.

Nevertheless, rebuilding in replica can have an important, albeit limited, role in making townscape: for instance, to complete or restore a formal architectural urban design concept; or again, to recreate an existing building which genuinely cannot be retained for structural or other reasons, but is of benefit to the visual character of the area.

Occasionally, grand architectural

concepts have not been completed as originally intended due to financial constraints [4.13]. After more than 150 years, the setting for this majestic university building has at last been satisfactorily completed. The flanking replica pavilions, finished in Portland stone and laid in ashlar blocks, are hardly distinguishable from the adjoining terraces. The entrance lodges have been enlarged and repositioned to complete the pleasing effect.

In certain situations, reconstructing an existing building in replica may be positively undesirable when considered from the townscape point of view. It is generally accepted as appropriate to make strenuous efforts to preserve buildings of intrinsic historic or architectural interest, irrespective of the relationship they form with their context. But if such a building cannot be retained, a conscious decision has to be made as to whether or not a new development should replicate it [4.14]. This is a splendid

4.12

4.13

example of faithful reconstruction: the repetition of the different glazing pattern on the top floor increases the sense of authenticity; and the opportunity has been taken to introduce period shopfronts of real quality. However, when considered in its context, this building is not characteristic and in scale with adjoining buildings. An opportunity has been lost to create a '1980s' building that unites the townscape. Instead, a 1980s structure repeats the appearance of the 1830s for no apparent reason.

In a planned area, it is important to retain character by replicating buildings where necessary [*4.15*]. This end of terrace block forms one end of a symmetrical composition. It is commendable that the designer has resisted the obvious temptation to continue the mansard accommodation, as provided on the new extension on the left, across the replica block. This would have disturbed the symmetry and architectural integrity of the whole terrace.

Redevelopment

Where the local economy is buoyant, there will always be considerable impetus for redevelopment. Developers and conservative funding institutions have a distinct preference for total redevelopment, also the favoured option of architects, though with a few notable exceptions. To some extent this is understandable, as their education and motivation is geared towards designing new buildings rather than adapting and conserving existing fabric.

Redevelopment has an essential role to play in making townscape and in ensuring that areas remain alive and interesting. Indeed, it is desirable to have representative buildings of all periods, including our own. But to be acceptable and successful it needs to be undertaken on a far more selective basis. Redevelopment should be actively encouraged and channelled into locations where it will be most beneficial, whether for local employment, social considerations, or the local environment. It should be firmly steered away from situations where it would have a destructive effect. Too often, buildings and townscapes of real

4.14

merit and great potential have disappeared, whereas areas of poor environmental quality with little scope for improvement have survived. One encouraging trend is that the age of a building is no longer the automatic indicator of its life expectancy. Numerous Victorian and earlier buildings will outlive their 1960s and '70s counterparts, thus relieving, to some extent, the development pressure elsewhere.

In relation to making townscape, redevelopment provides opportunities to improve an area, even where the loss

of a building of some interest may be involved; there is a lesson here for planning authorities and local amenity groups alike. There is some justification in the oft-repeated accusation that there is a tendency to want to preserve existing structures for their age and sentimental attachment. This stems, in part, from a genuine fear that redevelopment will inevitably have negative results, whether because it involves the loss of a familiar landmark, or the displacement of existing uses and occupants. Local amenity groups can become blind to the fact that, for

4.15

example, Victorian buildings were sometimes brutal intrusions, introducing a quite alien scale and character to their context. In such a case, unless the building is of special architectural or historic interest, and sometimes even when it is, redevelopment should not be dismissed simply because of a natural desire to maintain the status quo. Of course this is said on the assumption, and it is a broad assumption, that such redevelopment would create positive change.

Selection of alternatives

This will necessarily depend upon the circumstances of the individual case; but it seems that the most successful schemes, assessed in urban design terms, result from a combination of the alternatives already considered—in contrast to the simplistic and sometimes brutal approach of flattening part of a town, or a particular site, and starting again. Indeed, to create truly

successful townscapes, both functionally and aesthetically, complexity is usually an essential ingredient.

The final strategy adopted will depend upon a range of factors, and the effect on the townscape will be only one consideration. The thoughtful and responsive attitude advocated here, however, can have political as well as practical benefits. For instance, it demonstrates to the local community and their elected representatives that care and restraint have been exercised in drawing up proposals. It also shows that the existing character and value of the place have been assessed properly and avoids the impression sometimes given of a 'smash and grab raid'.

Both the developer and his designer should be sensitive to the natural, and understandable, apprehension local people will have towards redevelopment. Experience will have taught them that, almost without exception, the various changes that have occurred during the past few decades have

been for the worse. Much-loved areas and buildings, many with personal associations, will have been lost, to be replaced by generally mediocre new developments. The architectural profession has no one but itself to blame.

The general resistance that development proposals meet will be overcome only when designers and their clients appreciate the feelings, values and aspirations of local communities. Genuine steps should be taken to consult and involve the local people and to gain their understanding and support. This should never be approached as a superficial public relations exercise to stem any local opposition. While there may be a natural resistance to change in all of us, designers often underestimate the capacity of non-professionals to respond positively to good design and good townscape when it is on offer.

4.16

TOWNSCAPE IMPACT ANALYSIS

Introduction

A rigorous assessment of the effect of proposals on the locality concerned should be an integral part of the design process. Too often, it appears that spurious reasons are devised by designers to justify pre-conceived solutions. At present there is no specific requirement for an assessment to be made to accompany a planning application. Judging by some submissions, it is difficult to believe that the architect has ever visited the site. Application drawings frequently provide the minimum information and adjoining buildings are often barely shown. The aspects covered below under various headings are not intended to be comprehensive, but cover matters that are likely to affect most applications.

If the result of the assessment shows that certain aspects of the brief are likely to affect the townscape detri-

mentally, then this should enable the designer to raise them with the client and amend the scheme prior to submitting it for the local authority. Inevitably, it may well be impossible to satisfy all the criteria, but having conducted an impact assessment, at least the potential problems will have been highlighted at an early stage.

Visual impact

One obvious aspect which is continually being overlooked is the impact that new developments have on their surroundings. While it is now generally established that to relate new buildings to their context is a sensible, even desirable practice, little regard still appears to be paid to their wider effect on skylines and local views. This is partly a failure of designers, who naturally concentrate on the specific problems of erecting their scheme on a particular site. Certain shortcomings in their training can also lead to the

broader implications of their designs being overlooked. Planners and urban designers, on the other hand, have little room for complacency as they are directly responsible for assessing the wider impact of development proposals. So long as architects and planners persist in concentrating on individual sites and their immediate surroundings, plant rooms, for instance, will continue to crop up in the most unexpected views [4.16]. This example in a world-famous location is familiar to monarchs, heads of government and tourists alike. Unaccountably, a substantial white brick and lead-faced plant enclosure has been permitted to detract from the dignity of the arch which closes this impressive vista. It assumes a quite unacceptable prominence in what should surely be a protected view.

Longer views
Unlike aspects such as safeguarding the 'setting' of listed buildings, which

4.17

4.18

are given a broad official definition, there is no such specific requirement laid upon planning authorities to consider the impact of new proposals on views in their areas. Although a significant number of authorities clearly do take such considerations into account, generally speaking these views do not receive special protection. One of the few exceptions is the control operated within the City of London for over thirty years, known as St Paul's Heights, the purpose of which is to protect views of the cathedral and maintain its prominence on the London skyline.

Lesser-known buildings also deserve careful consideration [4.17]. Here, a new development has arisen behind a historic landmark, and blurs its silhouette. The subtle effect of the elegant dome belonging to this distinguished piece of eighteenth-century architecture has been lost, and its impact in terminating the approach across the bridge has been weakened. Tall

buildings continue to cause visual intrusion to an unacceptable degree [4.18]. In this famous view the striking development in the distance negates both the established scale and the sense of perspective. It also detracts from the setting of numerous listed buildings in the foreground.

When considering proposals which significantly exceed the height of the surroundings, the local planners should identify particular viewpoints at an early stage and invite the applicants to produce photomontages. These are likely to be far more reliable than the infamous and fantastic 'artist's impressions' or perspectives.

But developments do not have to be substantially higher than adjoining buildings to have an undesirable effect [4.19]. Some care has been taken to relate the scale of this large new development to its context when viewed in the street, by breaking down its length into different bays, and varying the eaves; but its true scale is

only too apparent when seen across an adjacent open space. This is emphasised by the monotonous and unified roof form.

Local views

While it may be understandable, if not excusable, that the impact on longer views can be overlooked, the fact that this also happens with more immediate views is far more disturbing [4.20]. The desire for many organisations to have a distinct identity can lead to difficulties and a break with the context. In this example, not only the bulk, but the general form and use of materials combine to create an overpowering impression. It has destroyed the richness and coherence of this once notable street. It is somewhat ironic, therefore, that, when constructed, it was the recipient of a prestigious environmental award.

It is puzzling how some schemes ever leave the drawing board [4.21]. The intimidating effect of this considerable

4.19

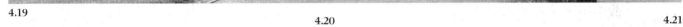

4.20

4.21

4.22

cantilever, violently intruding as it does into views up the hill, must have been readily apparent from the submitted drawings.

Street pattern

The historic development of our urban centres has resulted in street layouts typified by an irregular, closely-defined pattern, albeit overlaid with more recent interventions. The existence of such a street pattern should inevitably be a limiting factor on the size and scale of new development, no matter how many individual sites may have been assembled. This is especially true today, as the means of achieving the acquiescence of local communities to wholesale change by the promise of improved living conditions has long been exposed as a cruelly false dream. Indeed, achieving major inner road schemes or comprehensive redevelopments by the back door, in the name of 'slum clearance', is no longer socially

or politically acceptable. This is not to say that an existing pattern of streets should necessarily be sacrosanct and that radical departures cannot or should not take place [4.22]. The opening up of Westminster Cathedral from Victoria Street has been an outstanding success. It is an example of positive urban design, even though the Cathedral was designed to be viewed obliquely, and therefore does not address the new piazza formally. Ten years on, the massive office developments framing this now familiar view do not, judged by current standards, convey the desired sense of place. However, exposing monuments by adapting surrounding streets is not always desirable, particularly in our historic urban centres, where the element of surprise can be more exciting than the formalised, full frontal view.

There is often pressure to extinguish ancient streets and pedestrian routes, or to envelope them within

developments—taking them through covered atriums, for instance. This automatically transfers them from the public domain to become private, security-controlled environments. But it is possible to create successful sheltered pedestrian routes [4.23]. Shopping and commercial complexes form a very large ingredient in town centres, and, as such, offer considerable opportunities to improve, as well as threaten, the townscape. Here, an attractive, covered street has been formed which is more akin to the light and airy Victorian arcades still to be found in northern towns, rather than the dark, claustrophobic shopping malls of a decade ago. No doubt this is largely the result of rising expectations from more discriminating consumers.

Pressure may also be exerted to bridge over streets at upper levels, to provide links between different buildings in the same occupancy. While this does not alter the street pattern on the ground, it can radically alter, and not

4.23

4.24

4.25

always for the better, the appreciation of its spatial character [4.24]. This elevated link block also seriously detracts from the setting of a notable building.

Density and scale

Where the character of an area depends upon the juxtaposition of different scales, a general levelling up would tend to erode this specific sense of place, and so not be appropriate. However, where a site has previously been underdeveloped in relation to its surroundings, then an increase in scale on redevelopment would be desirable. The pressure will usually be to over-develop a site, or at least to achieve its maximum potential, although there may be exceptions [4.25]. A multiple retailer occupying a frontage in a shopping street may not wish to become involved in tenanting accommodation above his unit which is likely to attract a different use. Here, it has resulted in a suburban scale in the heart of town. In other locations, greater site rental values would dictate another form of development.

4.26

4.27

The built scale of our towns has been influenced by a number of restrictions and other factors, long before the introduction of the present development control procedures. Various building acts, and the practices of individual landowners, often resulted in specific requirements regarding heights, rights of light, use of materials and architectural detail. The relaxation of such controls towards the end of the last century, combined with technical innovations like the steel frame and the lift, led to a quite dramatic increase in the urban scale, only surpassed by the speculative developments of the '60s and '70s.

Scale is governed principally by height and plot size. A development can be in scale on its main street frontage, but have a very deep site forming the whole side of an adjoining side street [4.26]. This department store continues the irregular alignment which reflects earlier, smaller buildings once occupying the site. While its height and materials are appropriate for the area, it presents a very forbidding, never-ending face to the pedestrian, lacking display windows, or even downpipes which could have provided some relief.

New developments do not have to be very much higher than adjoining buildings for their difference in scale to be significant on the townscape [4.27]. In this typical street of a market town, two stories in excess of the norm introduces an overlarge scale. The use of a miniaturised podium and slab block form has created this distortion. It should have been possible to achieve the same accommodation on the site in a far less disruptive way. Indeed this is the case with most tower blocks, if the occupier and the local community is prepared, on redevelopment, to forego the much-trumpeted benefits of the surrounding 'SLOAP', which is usually occupied by car parking, or thoroughly unpleasant, scrubbily-planted amenity areas.

Traffic generation and parking provision

The last twenty years have witnessed a tremendous growth in personal transport, far exceeding official estimates. The devastation and physical severance caused by the construction of inner distributor roads, urban motorways, and what are euphemistically called 'highway improvements', have been the result of a vain attempt to accommodate the increase in the car population.

Increasing traffic movements represent a severe strain on urban life, and also have a fundamental effect on the character and amenity of neighbourhoods. It is generally accepted that to arrest the decline in inner-city residence, and to encourage more people to live centrally, is a desirable

4.28

[4.29]. In this type of location, where the surrounding scale is small and intricate, the simple geometry and stark outline of the traditional multi-storey would be visually unacceptable. Here, a complex sequence or roof forms has been manipulated to create a suitably fragmented roofscape. No doubt this approach can be criticised for being cosmetic, or even dishonest, but there can be no question that most people would find it infinitely prefer-able to the typical alternative. De-signers are now able to tackle the considerable challenge of placing a car park next to an elegant civic building [4.30]. In this case, the enriched façade of the car park successfully takes its place in the street scene. This is because the designer has produced a solution which stands scrutiny as a piece of urban architecture—something the Victorians would, no doubt, have appreciated. It is to be hoped that these will not remain

aim. But this must be combined with positive measures to protect the basic amenities of these areas. This can be partly achieved by resisting develop-ments likely to generate unacceptable increases in local traffic: a problem often directly related to large retail outlets that attract not only service vehicles, but car users as well.

Off-street car parking, whether in the form of surface parking or multi-storey car parks, has also had a major impact on our townscapes. The 'car stack', as it is sometimes known, is a building type unique to the late twentieth century. These have become so widespread that no decent-sized town is complete without one. Until recently, they could easily be identified by their familiar, utilitarian ap-pearance and box-like horizontal form. There are examples where this has been successfully softened by cloaking them with perimeter development [4.28]. This can greatly help the townscape by introducing interest and activity at street level. It is diffi-cult to imagine a more unpleasant townscape-experience than to walk past a conventional multi-storey. Another approach is to accept them for what they are and to integrate them architecturally with their context

4.29

4.30

4.31

isolated examples. They demonstrate that even incongruous building types can, given some care and imagination, play an acceptable part in the overall townscape.

Servicing

This can be potentially very damaging and disruptive, in terms not only of noise and pollution, associated with large delivery vehicles manoeuvring in confined spaces, but also the physical measures that have to be taken to accommodate them. These take various forms from street widening, large set backs and open service yards, to the creation of large gaping holes in the street frontage [4.31]. Such openings are inevitably unattractive, unkempt and even menacing. The size of this type of service entrance is dictated by the dimensions of goods vehicles. Unlike other European countries—Italy, for example—we have sought to alter our built environment to accom-

modate the largest delivery vehicles rather than adopt a style and scale of retailing which demands less bulk deliveries, and can therefore be adequately serviced by smaller vehicles.

Some multiple retailers appear almost to have a house style for service bays. These consist of anonymous brick boxes which visually smother the surrounding area and create an atmosphere of alienation [4.32]. Here, architecture is used as a medium for self-advertisement. It is interesting to speculate quite what image is being conveyed.

Large service areas are frequently formed to the rear of pedestrianised streets, thereby creating windswept, sterile, car-infested backlands, the disadvantage of which more than offsets any potential attractions of pedestrianisation for making good townscape. Service areas do not have to be unpleasant if some thought is given to their treatment [4.33]. In this atypical example considerable care is

evident both in the architectural design and the groundscaping, although unfinished when the photograph was taken. It can be contrasted with the other half of this particular area, which presents a more characteristic picture of oil-stained tarmac, battered roller shutters and huddles of smelly paladins.

These often large areas of backland, occupying a significant percentage of a typical urban block, could have considerable possibilities for creating new pedestrian routes. While the individual designer can produce magnificent schemes for service areas, local authorities have a vital role. Wherever appropriate, they should vary their standards to allow more flexibility. Above all, they should insist on the creation of off-street service areas only where these are essential. Apart from the obvious environmental damage they cause, they are frequently not used for their intended purpose and become executive parking spaces.

Assessment and conclusion

The assessment of the impact of design proposals should be on-going throughout every stage of the design. In a specific situation, certain of the basic factors mentioned above will assume greater relevance than others. For instance, a site may lie within a famous local view and this will have an important influence on the final proposals, whereas, for an infill site, views may hardly be relevant. Clearly, when developing a small site, the wider impact is likely to be reduced. For large developments, most, if not all, of these aspects will be relevant.

When the townscape impact has been analysed and assessed, this will then have to be balanced against economic, employment and social considerations. It will depend on the particular circumstances as to which are given greater weight by the planning authority.

4.32

4.33

Chapter 5

CONTEXTURE: THE ACT OF WEAVING TOGETHER

When involved in any new development, the designer is primarily concerned, and understandably so, with the realisation of his concept, whereas the concern and responsibility of the planner, elected member or local community will extend far beyond this limited objective to encompass the local and wider public interest. These distinct, but parallel spheres of interest should be seen by all concerned as being complementary, rather than in conflict.

The attitude with which the designer and his client approach the question of building in an existing setting is crucial. It often seems that designers develop pre-conceived ideas and then try to justify them in terms of the local context. Sometimes it appears that ideas have been plagiarised from other architects or from the visually seductive pages of the architectural glossies. Alternatively, designers will produce an appropriate scheme for one site and then, rather than develop their ideas further, simply re-jig the 'winning formula' or house style, and provide virtually the same solution for quite a different context.

'Contexture', on the other hand, involves weaving together the old and the new to create a satisfying, living totality. This is in contrast to the all too familiar pot-pourri of discordant parts which shout at each other, rather than acting in harmony. The fundamental lesson that has to be learned, and re-learned, is that 'the place' is more important than any individual architectural conception, however meritorious. Once accepted, this discipline will lead logically to the recognition that old and new need to be related to

each other. When this sense of place is allowed to take precedence, its collective nature will need to be understood and underpinned. Change there must be—there is no question here of attempting to put the clock back or of setting a particular moment in aspic as being the 'ideal'—but change should not be negative and destructive, but rather directed to the positive and creative.

Contextualism is one of the 'buzz' words currently in circulation. As a result, a lot of lip service is being paid to context. Sadly, this sometimes cynical performance does not always alter or improve the end result. Any proposal should be judged on the evidence of the presentation drawings, and not by any supporting statement, however fluently presented.

This chapter sets out a logical approach to designing in an existing urban area. Wider aspects are first considered before we move on to more detailed factors. These finer architectural points may be thought by some to be beyond the scope of making townscape. But we feel it necessary at least to touch on them, as, so often, potentially successful buildings are seriously flawed by lack of attention and skill in their detailed design.

TOWNSCAPE ROLE

'Keeping in keeping'

The term 'keeping in keeping' is often used in a derogatory or dismissive sense to describe what some architects perceive as a timid conservationist attitude, stifling innovatory design and encouraging the commitment of the

ultimate sin, a pastiche. The latter is defined as a composition made up from various sources, or composed in the style of a known author. Using this definition, few so-called Modern buildings would escape such condemnation.

There is a clear inference here that the adoption of a contextualist approach is a temporary aberration imposed by planning authorities emboldened by the popular backlash against Modernism and the low public opinion of the architectural profession: that to propose such a course of action is to fly in the face of all historical precedent and commonsense. This argument is frequently coupled with the astonishing assertion that it results in works of great architecture being stillborn. Given that there have been only a handful of masters since the Renaissance, this claim hardly warrants serious consideration. Indeed, architects of the distinction of Hawksmoor and Holden have demonstrated their 'willingness' to recognise the wider claims of townscape and their respect for work of their predecessors in preference to their own egos.

In fact, there is plenty of evidence that this civilised practice is far from being an aberration. It may be helpful to quote some examples to disprove the fallacy that it is only twentieth-century architects who have, either as a result of external requirements, or through their own sensibilities, modified the predominant architectural expression of the day, or their personal style, when designing in specific locations [5.1]. This illustration represents nearly 1000 years of architectural history. The Tudor gatehouse, incorporating a

5.1

Norman archway, is overlooked by the Decorated West Front of the cathedral-sized church. When Charles Holden conceived his design for a new library in the early years of this century, he did not adopt his favourite mannered classicism, of which he was a leading exponent; instead, he created a composition that sits happily in its historic context and is yet fresh and original.

Certainly, it could not be mistaken for belonging to any other century than our own. It is relevant to note that he did employ the classical vocabulary for much of the interior, thus reinforcing the conclusion that he was consciously responding to the context as far as the exterior was concerned.

In many towns there is a dichotomy between the striking black and white

geometry of timber-framed buildings, and Georgian brickwork, which produces the familiar fragmented effect. But it is possible to produce an appropriate context for Tudor buildings without detracting from the integrity of the original [5.2]. Here, Edwardian half-timbering complements the magnificent surviving Tudor example on the left. The later buildings

5.2

5.3

5.4

combine to form an enclave with a particular visual unity. By taking up an existing theme, rather than introducing a new one, the architect has re-integrated the Tudor building into the townscape. Without this neighbourly gesture, it would have been out on a limb, like a museum piece.

There are many other examples of a later building helping to underline an existing character, rather than diversifying, which in a confined space would have been visually disruptive [5.3]. In a collegiate setting, the Victorian infill in the centre continues the scale and architectural form of its seventeenth-century neighbour in the foreground.

It is possible to provide a visual link between dramatically different building types where the situation demands it [5.4]. In this case, the mullioned staircase tower to an office development creates a reference to the mullioned Gothic windows of the church—a device which helps to soften

5.5

the otherwise stark contrast between these two buildings.

Sadly, not all attempts at respecting the context are particularly successful [5.5]. Here, the recent building appears to be a rather unhappy hybrid. The provision of jettied stories, without the essential vertical subdivision, emphasised by the pronounced gables of its neighbour, only serves to exaggerate the horizontality of the design.

Some current designs appear to be caricatures of adjoining buildings, often taking on a frivolous—or to employ the current jargon, 'ironic'—character. Yet their designers still expect their work to be taken seriously [5.6]. By his arbitrary introducton of gridded panels of brickwork, the architect appears to be making a clear reference to the adjacent brick and stone building in the foreground. But this abstract pattern-making amounts to little more than a fatuous gesture, trivialising the traditional architectural forms of the context, rather than creating a harmonious relationship.

Finally, on a much smaller scale, is the earliest example quoted here of keeping in keeping [5.7]. The ornate fifteenth-century gatehouse is complemented by the charming, white-

5.6

5.7

5.8

painted, early nineteenth-century interpretation of the Gothic style. The
outline of this domestic example also
reflects that of the western front of the
Abbey beyond.

Member of a group

What constitutes a group of buildings
is often disputed. For some time the
government has listed buildings for
their 'group value', which lends official
recognition to this townscape concept.

The familiar urban scene is generally
composed of sequences of individual
buildings. They may form a series
where each building is similar to the
preceding one. These will often be part
of an area built at roughly the same
time, possibly as part of an overall plan
and of a similar character and materials. Such locations may present the
designer with little scope for self-
expression, or indeed, rebuilding.

Alternatively, the street may comprise a collection of structures that
have certain common features—such
as general scale, plot widths and a
common architectural language—
which sit harmoniously together, yet
exist as a group of essentially individual buildings [5.8]. This sequence

5.9

has a formal character derived from the architecture of each of the components. The smallest building is the earliest member. Its porticoed façade successfully acts as an intermediary between C. R. Cockerell's famous Bank of England, which also forms a striking closure to the facing street, and the rest of the group.

Here, it is difficult to see how any of these interesting buildings could be replaced without disturbing the pleasing effect of the overall composition. Elsewhere, informal groups will often present considerable scope for the creation of an exciting new design, even within the inevitable constraints. Groups will almost invariably have stronger and weaker members, and it is assumed, all things being equal, that it is the weaker elements, either in architectural or townscape terms, which will be the most likely candidates for replacement. In any event, it will be essential to assess the relative contribution made by neighbouring buildings to the group as a whole, as well as that made by the one presently occupying the site in question.

Some locations will present an opportunity to create a building with

5.10

greater presence and to enhance the overall appearance of the group. In other cases a new design should continue to play a subservient role to an adjoining building of greater importance [5.9]. In this development, situated in one of London's earliest planned squares, the architect has made due reference to the classical character of the area, while producing an independent piece of architecture— an impression reinforced by his use of red brick in a generally yellow stock area. The flemish bond with snapped headers provides a convincing brick façade; and the introduction of stucco decoration conveys an appropriate sense of importance, allowing it to hold its own with the adjacent grand palazzo, without dominating its other more humble neighbours. One slight reservation is the relative weakness of the top cornice, which could have been better placed just above the head of the third floor window, while the mansarded top floor appears over-dominant, particularly in longer views from the square garden.

A site may lie between two areas with disparate uses and distinct townscape characters [5.10]. Here, the new development acts as a link between a typical Georgian street and a semi-industrial warehouse quarter enjoying a prominent riverside location. The designer has provided a suitable end stop to the terrace, before stepping down to address the river and adjoining series of warehouses. He has achieved this by changing the scale and fenestration in a convincing manner.

In other cases, whole streets can effectively act as a group, with each side having similar characteristics to reinforce the sense of unity [5.11]. The building on the left is one of the few recent developments in an otherwise complete piece of exuberant late-Victorian townscape. Featuring a nicely proportioned turret and subtly modelled brickwork, it performs as well as could be expected in townscape terms and completes the overall picture.

Where a strong visual pattern has been established, designers often appear reluctant to embrace whole-heartedly what they perceive to be

5.11

5.12

5.13

the restrictions imposed by the existing context. In doing so, they can fail to exploit them fully in a creative way [5.12]. While the upper level cleverly paraphrases its gabled neighbours, the introduction of brickwork and natural, rather than stained timber, mars an otherwise potentially successful member of this group. It is instructive to note that nearly three centuries separate its immediate neighbours.

If a new development will be seen as part of an existing cohesive entity, there is little option but to conform to the discipline that this imposes [5.13]. Fronting a large retailing complex, this recent end of terrace building shows a genuine attempt to relate it to the rest of the group. It expresses its corner location and provides an improved return façade; yet in spite of taking all the obvious steps—following through the eaves line, employing similar material and reflecting the arched window form—it sits somewhat un-

comfortably as an introduction to its neighbours. Even if accommodation was not required at second floor level, the well-tried device of blind windows could have provided the right scale and further articulation of the façade. The use of modish, Post-Modern, bas-relief decoration really is no substitute for the simple but vigorous Victorian detailing on the adjoining buildings. A further failing is the way in which the body of the new building is not supported by a visually adequate structure at ground level.

Juxtapositions

One of the most contentious areas of architectural debate today centres on what the appropriate design response is to the placing of a new building in an existing setting with an established architectural character.

The practice of keeping in keeping, not only in terms of architectural

character, but of scale and form as well, has already been discussed. An opposite approach, now somewhat in retreat, can perhaps best be defined as the 'total contrast', or 'negative statement', currently finding modish expression in the all-mirror-glass façade. The basic argument advanced for this approach to design is that the resulting architecture, if indeed that is what it can be called, is of our time and is neither 'in' nor 'out' of character. It does not attempt to compete with the existing townscape on its own terms. Instead, by setting up an often stark contrast, it highlights, and acts as a 'neutral' foil to the wealth of character and intricacy of Pre-Modern buildings, which is considered anachronistic in the closing years of the twentieth century.

To employ an artistic analogy, the rude juxtaposition of a Mondrian hung next to a Durer print [5.14] might just work in the confined and abstract environment of the modern art gallery, where the viewer is expected to appreciate works of art divorced from their contemporary context. But whether the practice can ever be translated successfully into built form is open to serious doubt.

Those who advance this view argue that to suggest their designs should reflect a sensitivity towards their context, and an awareness of the work of their predecessors, is in some way needlessly stifling their creativity. They also consider that they are being forced to accept an arbitrary discipline, enforced by mere 'geography graduates', which they believe is rooted in what they regard as the attitudes of the 'anti-anything' new conservationist lobby. It is ironic that these same architects have shown themselves the most eager to embrace wholeheartedly the severe design limitations imposed by the Modernist credo.

Clearly, some alarming juxtapositions have been created on the assumption, once commonly made, that all older buildings would eventually be redeveloped [5.15]. The difficulty with some sites is that they are almost incapable of redevelopment due to their size. So what in the 1960s may have been considered as a temporary situation has continued for thirty years. In the present climate, the '60s office 'slab' may be the first to go. Had the architect concerned been asked to relate to the adjoining Edwardian façade, he would, no doubt, have vigorously questioned the validity of respecting a building that he assumed would have a limited life. The simple answer would have been that, had he done so, the rate and impact of change would have been modified and the character and essence of the place would have survived. Incremental change has typified the long-term evolution of our urban centres. These have evolved at a pace where familiar scenes have developed gradually, thus avoiding the upheaval and sense of estrangement which many local communities have experienced in the wake of comprehensive redevelopments.

In other situations, architectural forms are employed that may be acceptable in themselves, but create unsatisfactory relationships when

5.14

placed next to an adjoining site [5.16]. Here, a stepped cantilevered façade introduces a cavernous void. In setting back the building at the lower levels the traditional sense of enclosure created by development on the back edge of the pavement has been lost.

The visual and physical fragmentation caused by these dramatic contrasts is all around us. Far from finding the resulting anarchy exciting and liberating, the onlooker may react in a

5.15

5.16

5.17

5.18

different way, by finding it all very disconcerting. Society is constantly being asked to assimilate new and often unfamiliar forms. Most of these are not seen in isolation, but are perceived as being sometimes violently juxtaposed with familiar images which tend, if anything, to heighten the shock of the new [5.17]. The casual visitor, browsing through the Victorian market, is abruptly confronted by this contained view of a structure which to most people is quite incomprehensible, and to some profoundly disquieting.

Placing a new extension next to a national monument can never be an easy task. Replica extensions are not necessarily successful as they can give the enlarged building a 'stretched' appearance. In addition, this solution effectively avoids the opportunity to create a positive juxtaposition. Faced with this challenge it may be difficult to avoid being inhibited and therefore producing a timid response [5.18]. The new wing is, if anything, more monolithic than its distinguished neighbour.

The problem of how to build next to an existing building with a distinctive architectural form and character will always be with us [5.19]. The success of this example, constructed in 1900, in relating to its fifteenth-century neighbour is remarkable, particularly as the designer did not resort to the use of overtly Gothic features. A satisfactory juxtaposition has been achieved by the conscious manipulation of horizontal and vertical elements, such as string courses, cornices, the faceted turret, and window proportions, which correspond closely to features on the church tower.

Divergence

Buildings that diverge from the general building line tend to be more conspicuous and, as a result, have an added opportunity for display. Such occasions may occur through a historic peculiarity in the street pattern, or by adaptations in the arrangement of neighbouring sites. But even where site frontages conform, ways of emphasising the building can still be found where this would be appropriate—by setting back, for instance.

The potential impact of divergence has long been recognised and exploited, although some more recent examples have been less successful. Indeed one of the most notable characteristics of post-war urban developments has been the systematic destruction of the legible street plan inherited from earlier periods. New buildings have tended to erode the clarity of traditional urban spaces as defined by building frontages sited on the back edge of the pavement.

Even relatively minor adjustments to an established building line can have an undesirable effect [5.20]. In this well-known example, the later central section of the Regency block has been arbitrarily removed. This has bisected it into two equal parts, robbing the terrace of the compositional cohesion required. Traditionally, entrances have been celebrated architecturally to give them prominence in the street. Here, the point of entry remains somewhat obscure.

Although some sites may not appear to project much in plan, they can be

5.19

quite pronounced when viewed obliquely [5.21]. Due to the position of the church, the flank wall of this unremarkable Georgian house is unusually exposed. Full advantage of the opportunity for display has been taken so that the return with curved bays has been given as much importance as the street façade.

Other sites may project more obviously and require an architectural response [5.22]. When a divergence in the building line is marked with skill and sensitivity, this can add richness and diversity to the townscape. In this example, a narrow site projects beyond its neighbour. The designer has exploited the possibility of giving the

5.20

5.21

5.22

small bank considerable presence, taking care to give importance to the exposed flank wall by installing a decorative balcony.

Overhanging upper floors can achieve prominence for a building, even if the ground floor conforms to the general building line [5.23]. But here there seems to be no valid reason for them. The oppressive projection of the recent extension to the elegant bank appears to overwhelm it in a quite unacceptable way and draws undue attention to itself. But breaking free

from the discipline imposed by building lines can be justified, particularly for buildings in public use [5.24]. In this instance, the monumental portico of the theatre bridges the pavement, providing much-needed shelter as well as a suitable visual marker in the street.

Just as projecting a building can enhance its importance, so equally can setting it back. Far from making it appear retiring, recession can lend a building an air of dignity by setting it apart from its neighbours. This can be

5.23

5.24

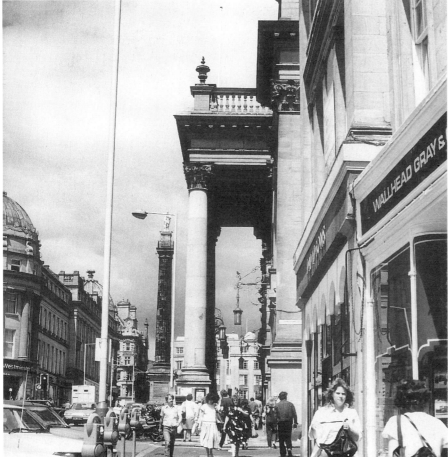

5.25

especially relevant in urban situations where continuously built-up frontages can make the distinction between different functions and uses difficult [5.25]. In this example, the chapel has been set back for the full depth of the adjoining terrace. The drastic effect has been softened somewhat by the slate-hung flank wall.

Setting back can enable buildings that are significantly larger than their neighbours to avoid appearing over-bearing or incongruous [5.26]. Here, the set-back also provides an oppor-

5.26

5.27

5.28

tunity to introduce projecting, heavily rusticated entrances which enhance the importance of this bank. It can also provide a much-needed space for people to congregate outside a public building in a constricted street [5.27]. This former corn exchange, now hopelessly compromised, was probably set back for that reason. It marks one entrance to an indoor shopping mall. At the time, someone had the commendable idea of retaining such an attractive piece of nineteenth-century street architecture. Sadly, this has resulted in the retained façade being isolated from a relevant context. It merely serves to highlight the debased architecture, so typical of commercial developments natonwide, which now frames it.

Like projections, set-backs do not always occur at ground level [5.28]. In this case the lower podium block conforms more or less to the height of adjoining buildings to the right and to the building line. Only part of the upper block is seen to diverge. This may have

5.29

been an attempt to disguise the bulk, or the result of light and air agreements. But whatever the cause it has created a most uneasy visual effect.

Closing views

Nearly all our towns and cities are built on the familiar irregular street patterns which have evolved through the preceding centuries. This frequently results in urban views being terminated almost accidentally. Yet it is surprising just how many designers in the past have recognised the possibility of increasing the prominence and importance of their buildings by closing a view in a positive way. In so doing, they have also given the whole street added significance [5.29].

This pattern contrasts with urban areas based on a grid plan, so commonly found in North American cities, where streets are experienced as seemingly endless perspectives. High buildings, in particular, if set back slightly from the street frontage, can be

5.30

5.31

accepted; their presence is noted, but is not given an opportunity to dominate. When transposed to a European context, towers have usually had disastrous and sometimes unforeseen results [5.30]. Due to the irregular historic layout, an otherwise unexceptional site assumes an unacceptable dominance. Tall buildings can mar whole areas of a city by negating the sense of perspective and effectively foreshortening local corridor views. At the same time, they belittle the established townscape scale.

Other sites can project into a corridor view, rather than fully closing it [5.31]. In similar situations, an informal or picturesque solution may well be the answer, rather than providing a symmetrical composition, only part of which would come into view. In this example, the roofscape has been exploited for its full scenic potential, and suggests something lying beyond, just out of sight.

Unfortunately, there are still far too many instances where little, if any, serious attention appears to have been

given to the role of a building in closing a view [5.32]. In this internationally famous space, a side street is axially situated on its western side, opposite the mother of parliaments. The considerable potential for enhancing the townscape and providing a suitable link between the two imposing buildings fronting the square has been lost. Instead, the new development presents its rump to the square and does not give the impression of housing a major government facility.

Sites can often straddle the width of a street, so that only part of their frontage actually closes the view. In such cases, it may be possible to place the entrance or a staircase in such a way that the building can respond formally to its townscape role [5.33]. It should be noted that in this example the skyline has also been dramatised, increasing the impression of a positive reaction to an exposed location. The roofscapes of such buildings are visible to a far greater extent than is normally the case in built-up areas, and inevitably assume more prominence.

5.32

5.33

5.34

5.35

Excrescences such as plant rooms, if not carefully integrated into the design, can become the unwelcome focus of attention.

It is also possible to provide an appropriate visual stop while introducing incident to the street frontage running at right angles. This marks the fact that a building is performing a dual role [5.34]. Here, the white gable in the centre also closes the view [5.35]. Forming part of a much larger development, this gable with its centrally-placed upper window provides just the right degree of emphasis, while still clearly belonging to a secondary street. As an extension to a major clearing bank, it is a commendable example of a change in character and scale from the principal façade to a more vernacular style which reinforces the intimate ambience of the pedestrian route.

5.36

Turning corners

The art of turning corners was an aspect of architectural design much practised by Victorian and Edwardian builders, and one which they particularly enjoyed exploiting [5.36].

By contrast, the design of corners in the Georgian period was constrained, and subservient to a more formalised concept of architecture. The development of the 'free classical' style in the later nineteenth century allowed greater scope for innovation. Banks and public houses were often located on corner sites to give them prominence, and architects responded to their clients' aspirations by developing the stylistic freedom to stress their importance still further.

The designers of post-1945 buildings seem largely to have opted out of turning corners altogether. The Modern style precluded any special emphasis being given to corners. This, together with an unquestioning adherence to the rigid discipline of the structural grid, has resulted in a commonplace and monotonous angularity, which to some extent echoes the elementary geometry of their Georgian predecessors. There are many different ways of celebrating corners and creating stimulating visual effects, and these should be encouraged wherever they may fit the design of a building and enhance the townscape.

5.37

5.38

continuing the window pattern, cornices and other features around the corner, a dramatic effect can be achieved [5.39]. Here, additional interest has been introduced by a decorative hierarchy differentiating each level, unlike the next example [5.40], where each projecting upper storey is of a similar pattern, apart from the inverted fenestration on the top floor. The overall impression is very striking, if somewhat restless.

Flowing corners
A flowing corner can be defined as a situation where the whole building frontage forms the corner. The gentle curve of the street can be given added emphasis by using simple features such as a projecting eaves line [5.41]. The point where the two streets merge is hardly perceptible. The reverse situation of a concave, internal corner, being less familiar, can be quite dramatic [5.42]. The strong curve of the street is reinforced by the unbroken line. But just following the curve of the street around a bend does not automatically guarantee success [5.43]. The cut-away ground floor, reduced scale and horizontal emphasis create an unsatisfactory corner building, unsuited to its prominent townscape role and more traditional neighbours.

Hinged corners
The hinge can be a neutral method of linking two frontages at the corner which still allows them to predominate, rather than the corner itself. While this treatment can be applied to any angle, obviously the more acute it is the more prominent the hinge will become. Additional linkage can be achieved by carrying cornices and string courses around the corner, which produces a unified effect where two distinct frontages are keyed in [5.37]. To make a convincing hinged corner, this feature should ideally begin from ground level [5.38]. However, due to the acuteness of this corner, the jettied upper floors and the change in materials and fenestration, the hinge has been over-emphasised. It is divorced from the body of the building to such an extent that it hardly performs a connecting role.

Wrapped corners
Wrapped corners are a means of negotiating a corner without changing gear architecturally. Nevertheless, by

5.39

5.40

5.42

5.41

5.43

5.44

5.45

A corner can be enhanced and a building and its function highlighted by its architectural treatment [5.44]. Although this bank is no larger than its immediate surroundings, the classical idiom, with a heavily-expressed entablature supported by caryatids, increases its grandeur and strengthens the flowing corner.

Negative corners

Many corners of post-war buildings have either been denied entirely or cut back to form re-entrants. While some may have arisen from highway engineers' sight lines, others have re-sulted from a decision not to turn a corner in a positive way, but simply to butt two façades together [5.45]. Here, the effect of the cut-away corner is exaggerated by the height of the development. The introduction of such an uncharacteristic feature creates an additional visual interruption along the street frontage.

Elsewhere, designers have ignored the question of turning a corner altogether, with often disastrous consequences for the townscape [5.46]. The unsightly situation here appears to have arisen from meeting the need for access, leaving an exposed flank wall where a solid corner would have been expected.

Skyline emphasis

Giving emphasis to the silhouette of corner buildings has been one of the most appealing and successful ways of turning corners in the past. Vertical impact on a corner can be achieved by extending the building façade to make a strong elevated feature [5.47]. This unusual example is enhanced by the deeply projecting eaves.

Alternatively, the emphasis need not flow from the façade as a natural extension, but can be added above the main cornice level and still achieve an impressive effect [5.48].

Too much impact when turning a corner into a minor street can be disruptive [5.49]. The Space-Age chamfered top, although matching the pitch of adjoining roofs, forms an arresting and ungainly feature on the skyline. It is possible to find examples where a serious attempt has been made to give recent buildings an interesting corner which evokes the flavour of their surroundings [5.50]. While the corner turret echoes that of its neighbour, it is overscaled and lacks subtlety. The double height cut-away

5.46

5.47

5.48

5.49

5.50

individuality of different building types has been submerged to such an extent that they have become almost indistinguishable. A magistrate's court can appear like a theatre, while modern hospitals can look as anonymous and unwelcoming as an office block. As a direct result of the theories of the Modern Movement as practised in Britain, this destructive trend has decodified our townscapes. The loss of imagery incurred makes it difficult to identify building functions readily and has led to the visual impoverishment of our urban areas, once renowned for their richness. Traditionally, post offices have had a distinctive and dignified character which singled them out as public buildings; but with the development of communications, the letter post no longer enjoys the standing it once had [5.51]. In this situation, the post office also performs a townscape role in closing the view down the facing street. It is self-effacing, both in terms of its diminutive scale, which exposes the lightwell façade behind, and its reflective mirror-glass treatment.

It is to be hoped that the different building types and the functions they perform will once again be expressed in a positive way that will improve the legibility of our towns. Opportunities will then be provided for designers to create lasting works of architecture, comparable with the rich legacy of preceding centuries.

Civic

The great heyday for civic architecture came with the foundation of our present system of local government in the nineteenth century. The collection of Victorian town halls, public libraries, baths and other civic buildings, many of which hark back to the civic virtues of classical antiquity, greatly enlivens our townscapes. Some of them may not be very beautiful, yet they are much-loved and provide a focus for community life [5.52]. This town hall spire provides a strong visual marker and also tells the time; the adjacent, rather brutish extension, typical of the 1960s concept of civic architecture, conveys nothing of the dignity and self-esteem of its neighbour.

ground storey lends no visible means of support to the projecting turret, and, like that in the previous example, presents a somewhat menacing feature to pedestrians below.

BUILDING FUNCTION AND EXPRESSION

There are various reasons why a particular building should assume greater dominance in its setting, whether this is achieved by its having a larger scale or featuring different materials, or by an uncharacteristic form of architectural expression. One justification for this may be its specific townscape role, in acting as a focal point, for example, or turning a corner. Alternatively, it may stand out from its context because of its public function or the role of its occupier. Clearly, if it plays a significant part in the life of the local community, whether public, religious or cultural, then the building itself should express that role.

During the last few decades, the

5.51

5.52

5.53

Ecclesiastical

Historically, religious buildings have been the most instantly recognisable of all building types. Their central role has been expressed exuberantly in their architecture: steeples and spires have added greatly to our streetscapes and skylines. Particular denominations have even employed their own specific styles, legible to the initiated.

Churches have not always been set apart from their surroundings by a burial ground [5.53]. In this case the church forms part of the street frontage. Its idiosyncratic steeple provides enough of a visual clue to its function, without overpowering its domestically-scaled neighbours.

Contemporary religious architecture, on the other hand, appears to reflect a certain ambivalence about the role of the Church in a secularised society [5.54]. While this building is distinctive, it is not discerned as having a specifically religious use, even of the non-conformist variety. It illustrates a changing self-image and the current emphasis on pastoral and associated activities. Less ambiguous religious forms are gradually becoming part of the urban scene [5.55]. Ethnic minorities are finding scope for self-expression which signifies their growing influence in many inner-city areas. Here it is unfortunate that the dramatic silhouette that this recent mosque presents is partially obscured by the adjacent slab block.

Culture and entertainment

Theatres and opera houses are a long-established and characteristic building type. Their appearance provides a clear indication of their use, especially those constructed during the boom years of the last century [5.56]. This example, with its playful use of classical themes, looks just what it is—a venue for entertainment, a place for enjoyment—whereas the impression conveyed by its remarkable extension does not overtly suggest a theatre. The title of the play being staged when the photograph was taken, *Not quite Jerusalem*, is a fitting epithet for this and so many other recent cultural and entertainment complexes.

The cinema is a distinct twentieth-

5.54

5.55

5.56

century building type, which enjoyed its heyday as the home of the escapist fantasies of the depressed 1930s [5.57]. Many chains had strong corporate identities, but in the context of this small town the designer displays a remarkably restrained touch, yet clearly exploiting the exposed site and expressing a distinct function.

Commercial

In certain cases commercial buildings, such as the headquarters of a national organisation which may have a long association with a particular town, can rightly assume some prominence in the townscape. Indeed this can assist in providing a focus and sense of identity for the surrounding area. But in most cases, large-scale speculative developments and associated car parks have been the most disruptive forms of development. They have been allowed to achieve a quite unacceptable visual dominance to the detriment of most of

5.57

5.58

our towns and cities [5.58]. Here, the massive block of offices completely overpowers the surrounding area, including the town hall in the middle distance.

Shopping centre developments have been a major catalyst for change. Most of the earlier developments totally ignored their surroundings, both in terms of their apparent scale and in architectural form [5.59]. The second generation shopping centres reflect changing tastes and consumer aspirations, and have tended to go 'up market', leaving the lower end to the out of town or suburban discount warehouses. The more recent complexes are rather more contextural, even at the risk of sometimes appearing kitsch. Another change is that multiple retailers no longer necessarily own their sites, and therefore their corporate identity is often limited to shopfronts and signs, and does not extend to the architecture [5.60]. Corporate images have been a particularly damaging influence on the appearance of our townscapes. They have been applied nationwide, without any discrimination, unless required to show it by a handful of courageous local authorities.

Inevitably there will be some building types, and perhaps car parks are one of the most obvious examples, which, because of their inherent form and functional requirements, are likely

5.59

5.60

5.61

5.62

to be damaging to established built environments [5.61]. Their almost uniform horizontal emphasis, in this case modified by the close rhythm of vertical slots providing glimpses of the cars beyond, is visually detrimental and tends to destroy street frontages. It will often be necessary, especially in areas with an established character, to disguise them in order to minimise their impact [5.62]. Here a large multi-storey has been set back from the street, allowing another use, in this case housing, to form the outer wrapping.

RELATIONSHIP OF ARCHITECTURAL ELEMENTS

Elemental scale

Building scale, as has already been said, is a concept which is often bandied about in architectural and planning circles, yet is rarely defined or, apparently, understood. Department of Environment circulars make it clear that a development which is out of scale or character with its surroundings should not receive consent. But this does not imply that, provided a new development is not too large, it will automatically be acceptable. Scale in this primary sense has two specific ingredients: the overall perceived height, and the size of the plot; in other words it is a combination of vertical and horizontal dimensions.

While a proposal judged by these broad criteria may be satisfactory, the actual form of the design and the way in which it is articulated can dramatically alter its apparent scale, in both the primary, and the secondary sense.

It is generally accepted that the bulk of new developments should relate to their neighbours, at least as far as the street frontage is concerned. But that is as much as some designers appear to be prepared to concede; indeed, some argue that development control should be allowed to intervene no further [5.63]. Yet here is a classic demonstration of the need for such control of more detailed aspects of design. The fenestration, if that is what it can be called, gives little clue to the number of floors lurking behind the vertical, brick-clad prongs fronting the

5.63

5.64

It could even be said that the structural grid creates a sub-division which reflects the width of a typical town house. But the connecting bands of windows emphasise the horizontal scale, thereby setting it against the established grain of the area.

There are even more extreme examples [5.65]. Having carefully lined through, almost precisely, with the cornice of its classical neighbour, the designer then proceeded to produce an externalised skeletal structure. This provides the building with only one scale, running for virtually its full height; with the unfortunate result that, in spite of its relatively modest bulk, it appears to dwarf its larger neighbour.

A similar result can occur at a much smaller scale [5.66]. Although here the eaves height is the same, the new building is apparently much larger than its neighbours and of a different scale altogether. The fenestration, and in particular the jettied top storey, were presumably introduced to bring some interest and modelling to the façade. Yet when compared with the modest bays on the adjoining building, these elements are overscaled and appear to be leaning into the street.

curtain walling. These insistent un-broken vertical features exaggerate the height of the building and introduce a discordant role.

In the past, the in general vertically proportioned fenestrations were counterbalanced by strong horizontal elements such as band courses and cornices. With few exceptions,

pre-1950s buildings displayed this harmonious balance. Since then, designers have increasingly tended to opt for one emphasis or the other, resulting in assertive, restless compositions which sit uneasily in traditional townscapes [5.64]. The vertical scale of this building is compatible with that of the adjoining stuccoed terraces.

5.65

5.66

Bay-to-bay

The sequential way in which the townscape is perceived is an important factor to be taken into account during the design process. Ordinarily, the viewer first takes in a range of buildings from a particular viewpoint, and only then focuses on individual buildings, examining each in turn. It is the relationship of architectural elements at their junctions which either arrests the eye, or establishes a smooth visual transition between one building and another.

New buildings can be of a similar scale, colour or height and yet still contribute to the general fragmentation of townscapes that has occurred in most of our urban centres. Often, near-misses can be almost as disruptive as those buildings which make no attempt to relate to their context. The fundamental changes in the way in which buildings are constructed today, coupled with different uses and spatial requirements, pose particular challenges. This is especially so for any designer who is concerned to ensure that his work will eventually mature and merge with the surrounding scene.

One of the most intractable problems to overcome is the external effect of the provision of what are currently considered to be acceptable floor to ceiling heights, allied with the tremendous expansion of service requirements. The accommodation of these, in suspended ceilings and raised floors, can exert a strong influence on the exterior and thereby threaten established character, firstly, by creating a disparity between neighbouring and new floor levels, and secondly, through the consequential reduction in the scale of the fenestration [5.67].

The stone-faced façade of this recent building is highly modelled with deeply recessed windows. Yet when compared to its classically mannered neighbour, the crudity with which this has been achieved is all too apparent. It also lacks any secondary detailing, which could have assisted in establishing a more harmonious relationship.

5.67

Case studies

The following studies are intended to illustrate the degree of decorative complexity which can be required in certain situations in order successfully to place a new building in an existing street. The tentative use of the stylistic freedom that has emerged in the wake of the Modern Movement, together with a re-awakening of interest in our heritage by the architectural community, and their desire for experimentation and innovation, make the future enrichment and repair of our townscapes a real possibility.

Cornhill, London EC3

Cornhill is an atypical street in the City, in so far as it has not suffered from any Modern incursions and therefore possesses a special cohesion. The only other post-1945 structures have been timid one-bay replica façade extensions that have contributed nothing to the street and have been cowardly in design.

This infill site, joined on either side by very distinctive and richly ornamented buildings, posed a particularly interesting architectural and townscape challenge. The right balance has been struck, with the designer not being intimidated by the surrounding context, nor attempting to outdo neighbouring architecture. In creating the illusion of an ancient palazzo

5.68

5.69

belonging to a merchant prince, the architect has produced what the site required. And yet it is also a distinguished example of current architecture, and very much of our time. It has been designed with oblique views especially in mind [5.68]. The vigorous surface modelling can be readily appreciated; and the careful balance between the different emphases provided by the projecting vertical and horizontal elements should be noted.

The main cornice links through with that belonging to the building on the left [5.69]; while the base height and projecting course between first and second floors reflect those on the building to the right [5.70]. Setting up these direct relationships has been crucial in weaving in the new with the old [5.71].

The immense height of the ground floor has been necessary to provide a correct scale for the street, enabling a

5.73

5.74

5.70

5.71

5.72

mezzanine level to be installed, well set back from the frontage [5.72].

Piccadilly, London W1
The architects for this mid-1970s building had an equally challenging site and employed a similar technique, of creating comparable elements to relate specifically to adjacent buildings, while at the same time producing a façade which also stands scrutiny in its own right [5.73].

From the left-hand building, it has taken the impressive granite-faced plinth, striking horizontal banding and mullioned windows [5.74]; while from that on the right, it has borrowed the arched form of the first floor arcade from the exotic entrance to the Burlington Arcade [5.75]. This subtle blending has resulted in a design, appropriate to its important site, that has already begun to merge with the older fabric. A feature worthy of

particular note is the ingenious way in which the designer has inserted an additional floor between the plinth and cornice line. This has been achieved by creating a framework of mullions and transoms which effectively disguises the meanness of present-day office accommodation. The line of windows serving this intermediate level in fact reads as the floor line between first and second levels [5.76].

5.75

5.76

5.77

5.79

5.78

5.90

5.91

5.92

account of how they will be viewed obliquely from the street [5.91]. On the face of it, this development does the correct thing with its gigantic, two storied base, and piano nobile expressed above. However, the introduction of such direct visual relationships only helps to highlight the inherent two-dimensional character of the recent building in the foreground, which appears quite denuded and lacking in any secondary detailing, in this instance a critical factor.

Yet lining through is introduced even where a new design makes no other concessions to its context [5.92]. The way the top line of the curtain walling picks up the principal cornice line of the block seems to be more than a coincidence. Given the clash of architectural expression, such a device can only be an irrelevant gesture.

Storey heights and elevational hierarchy

The external manifestation of floor to floor heights has a major influence on the character of the resulting fenestration. One particular difficulty in relating a new building to a traditional townscape is the disappearance of the need to express an internal spatial hierarchy, once reflected by the familiar tripartite arrangement of base, middle and top. With the widespread

5.93

within the brickwork section of the façade, are similar in height. This is a shortcoming that could have been easily overcome by an enrichment of the architraves surrounding the first floor openings.

The increased expectations for a better working environment in offices, together with a general requirement for more sophisticated technical servicing, often results in the need for raised floors and suspended ceilings to accommodate the consequential equipment. These voids, created above and below the structural floors, could and should be used to facilitate variations in floor to floor heights. This would not only allow for different window sizes, but would also assist in relating new floor levels to the fenestration of retained façades.

A marked reduction in spatial requirements has had dramatic results, even at the modest scale, during the last 40 years or so [5.94]. This is a classic example of the incontrovertible truth: that three into two will not go. Perhaps, by the use of vertical bays, the designer hoped to diffuse the unavoidable horizontal comparison between respective window openings and the number of storeys they represent. This practice was also used to satisfy planning authorities that an appropriate bulk was achieved, consistent with the height of neighbouring developments. It was particularly preva-

adoption of current management philosophy, the managerial stratum may no longer expect or require to be housed in lofty rooms, preferring rather to encourage corporate identity.

However, for over 200 years, most buildings have been designed to reflect a definite hierarchy with a tall, imposing ground floor, introduced partly for other functional reasons, most importantly the provision of natural light and ventilation. This level was surmounted by a recognisable *piano nobile*, or principal floor [5.93]. The Georgian façade displays a dramatic reduction in proportion between the first and second floor windows—an effect increased by the addition of pediments over the former. By contrast, the windows at these respective levels in the new building, contained

5.94

lent in the heady days of the 1960s, when standards were pared down to the absolute minimum in order to maximise floorspace content. Ironically, it has produced an unexpected and much-welcomed bonus: many buildings of that distraught period have become prematurely outdated, as they are incapable of satisfying present, let alone future, needs, thus providing considerable scope for improvement.

An alternative to facing up to the problems of relating often disparate storey heights is to avoid the issue altogether [5.95]. By creating a uniform grid, the number of storeys is effectively disguised, at least during daylight hours. This creates an impression of complete anonymity, enhanced by the ubiquitous use of reflective glass. It is often contended that such designs are applicable to a wide variety of locations, just because of their blandness, whereas, in fact, buildings of this character are quite assertive and are rarely introduced successfully into our townscapes.

Traditionally, the internal hierarchy of buildings was indicated not only by the relative scale of each floor and its fenestration externally, but also by variations in the system of architectural decoration employed [5.96]. While the new building, which incidentally is an extension, reflects each level of the retained façade, there is no sense that one level is more significant

5.96

5.95

than another. This makes the lining through of floor levels a rather hollow contextural gesture.

Within the constraints imposed by current standardised floor to floor heights, there are also other ways in which a stultifying end result can be avoided [5.97]. By introducing a network of mullions and transoms, the architect has avoided the monotonous regularity of the adjacent buildings and has created the impression of a *piano nobile*, with the actual second floor being obscured behind the glazing. This provides a convincing elevational hierarchy.

The traditional plinth associated with the classical idiom created a unity, particularly when viewed from street level [5.98]. The prominent cornices, defining the double height

ground floors of the monumental bank buildings, pick up the entablature of the single storey screen wall on the left. This relationship is so strong that it overcomes the tremendous disparity in their relative sheer heights.

Doors

The point of entry into a building has traditionally been emphasised in a way that has left little doubt as to its location. Doorways were also used to express the wealth and status of the occupant, as well as introducing incident and interest to the street.

By contrast, Modern buildings have frequently failed to provide this essential visual information. They are often entered via an endless bank of identical glass doors, most of which have to be

5.97

5.98

5.99

tried before access is finally gained. Multiple entry points are no longer generally practicable with the current increase in security surveillance.

Doorways have been exploited for their decorative potential, even on otherwise quite plain buildings. Indeed during the Georgian period, architectural detail was concentrated almost exclusively upon the entrance [5.99]. This recent example is a witty re-working of classically inspired elements, introduced as part of a refurbishment of an eighteenth-century group, to which the steps add an extra flourish.

At the opposite end of the scale, the entrance to this major office complex seems to have been deliberately tucked away in the bottom right-hand corner [5.100]. Perhaps the architect was so enthralled by the gridded geometry of his fenestration that, for him, to have allowed the entrance to interrupt it would have been unthinkable.

There are welcome signs of a gradual return to celebrating entrances, which can be both visually stimulating and perform a useful function [5.101]. Yet there still appears to be a puzzling reluctance among designers to specify doors which exceed the standard height, especially when it is an accepted fact that the population as a whole is getting steadily taller. Here, though, the mouse-hole appearance has been largely mitigated by the large-scale window above, announcing the entrance in a quite emphatic style.

Windows

Windows, similarly, have tended to be played down in recent years. They are often expressed as little more than holes in the wall of a building, or, alternatively, denied altogether and submerged in a sea of darkly tinted or reflective curtain walling [5.102]. To the external viewer, such developments give few clues as to the activities taking place behind their anonymous grids, lending them an almost sinister

5.100

5.101

character. The introduction of large areas of reflective glass has been one of the most unwelcome, visually disruptive and aggressive innovations in architectural design for some time.

Part of the present situation can be traced directly to advances in air-conditioning and artificial lighting, which mean that, for certain building types, windows are now virtually redundant as sources of fresh air and light. The result is that the fundamental requirements influencing window design throughout preceding centuries no longer apply.

When designing in certain contexts, there will be little choice but to conform to the established window pattern and type, in order to produce a successful overall result [5.103]. Here it may appear that the designer did only the bare minimum in order to comply with such a requirement. However, on its completion in the 1960s, this small infill building, which continues the stone mullioned theme in concrete, was roundly condemned for even daring to go this far in respecting its neighbours. Indeed, the client body were chastised for their conservatism. Perhaps they were ahead of their time.

During discussions on architectural design criteria, catch-phrases such as 'solid and void', or 'hole in the wall' are common. It is salutary to note that some of the resulting designs are

5.102

5.103

5.104

5.105

5.106

literally that [5.104]. No attempt has been made to vary the windows and provide a visual hierarchy expressed by their proportion and detailing. The use of ubiquitous dark bronze framing teamed with darkly tinted glass (hardly a functional requirement given the diminutive scale of the openings), only increases the stark effect. It also illustrates another all too familiar shortcoming, the lack of reveals, which traditionally supplied visual weight and a three dimensional character to the window wall.

However, it is often unnecessary, except in a streetscape of definite consistency, for the new windows to be closely influenced by the established pattern. The overall personality of a building is created by a combination of features and these by themselves may be adequate to provide suitable linkages [5.105]. The new building on the left has an almost playful quality introduced by the sinuous curves. The

gently rounded bay at third and fourth levels begins at the point where the three storied bay of its individualistic neighbour terminates. The variation in window proportion, combined with surface banding, helps to establish the right visual references, without resorting to imitation. This is not an easy task given the dramatic contrast between brick and stucco.

The perceived scale and proportion of window openings can be significantly altered by their appropriate subdivision. Subdivided glazing, which was once considered an integral part of the overall design, has declined as a common feature over the past 60 years. Glass was originally introduced in small panes because of the prohibitive expense of larger sheets. However, the development of plate glass towards the mid-nineteenth century hastened the removal of glazing bars; though tentative steps are currently being made to reintroduce subdivision [5.106]. The

5.107

widespread use of sealed double-glazed units does, however, create practical difficulties. As the recent development on the right demonstrates, the usual compromise is for any subdividing glazing bars to be placed on the face of the glass. This can have an effect similar to the grids of white tape often used to give a Dickensian flavour to plateglass shopfronts at Christmas.

Another factor which can militate against the creation of elegant well-proportioned windows is the change from iron and timber to aluminium. Due to the inherent characteristics of the latter material, typical window sections are unduly heavy. They have a very simplified, flat external profile, which only increases their ungainly appearance. It is possible to introduce a secondary section, planted onto the outer face, in order to break down their width and introduce some shadow lines [5.106]. In addition, a darker colour was introduced here for the subframes, further to reduce the apparent width of the framing to the upper replacement windows on the left. Again this is a compromise and, ultimately, a more satisfactory and less cosmetic solution may be found by the manufacturers.

STRUCTURAL EXPRESSION AND BUILDING CONSTRUCTION

The way in which the structure of a building is to be expressed is a central question for designers. This must be the case, particularly with the current changes in direction of architecture, coupled with the inherent contradictions arising from the divorce of the outer skin of buildings from their structure. However, unlike their predecessors who elevated such issues to a high moral plane, designers in the more pragmatic post-Modern era need not perceive this as such a serious dilemma. Indeed the relative freedom allowed by the omnipresent structural frame can be exploited to produce buildings compatible with a contextualist approach.

It should be said that there is nothing new or essentially wrong about the concept of designing buildings as street architecture, as façades, even where these do not strictly accord with their

5.108

internal planning or structure.

With the development of new structural techniques, it is possible to introduce quite startling effects. But structural gymnastics can be very threatening and disconcerting to the unsuspecting passer-by, particularly when confronted by gravity-defying spans or cantilevers. Such exhibitionism is often visually disruptive when introduced into areas where most of the existing frontages take a load-bearing form, real or apparent

[5.107]. The designer of this strange building paid lip service to the planned, early nineteenth-century context. It is provided with a rusticated base, and punctured, load-bearing walls on the upper three storeys, complete with hierarchical fenestration, and vestigial cornice. These are seen to be supported miraculously by a continuous horizontal strip of glass.

The use of the structural frame, whether of steel or concrete, since its introduction in the early years of this century, has led to a fundamental change in the appearance of our townscapes. For the first few decades following its arrival, the structural frame was clothed in the richly modelled, monumental stone façades of the period, and thus there was no visual dichotomy between traditional load-bearing construction and framed buildings.

In the late 1950s, with the advent of curtain walling, the external face of buildings was reduced to a thin cladding system—the thinner the better in order to provide the maximum floorspace. At this time, the thickness of walls was included in calculations to determine the permissible area on each site; structure was obscured by a thin veil.

Since then, structural expressionism has made a somewhat uneasy comeback. In the absence of the discipline imposed by the laws of gravity and an accepted architectural language, designers have tended to lose their way [5.108]. An inevitable confusion arises here, as an intermediate column, which is given the same visual weight as its structurally integral neighbours, can be curtailed to provide access to the service bay. These columns are expressed as a series of match-sticks applied to the building face with little logic or integrity.

The articulation of the structural grid can be an effective way of breaking down the scale of a street frontage into manageable proportions, although it can also lead to an over-emphatic or repetitive result. While this may be appropriate to principal façades, when it is continued around the building, where it may enclose narrow side streets, the bay can appear grossly out of scale.

The face which the majority of recent developments presents to the outside world is essentially a veneer fronting a concrete sub-structure or, alternatively, hung from a steel frame. It is hardly surprising that the resulting architecture tends to have a flimsy, two-dimensional quality [5.109] (although this is not inevitable, as examples quoted elsewhere demonstrate).

This lack of depth is especially obvious where the cladding consists of

5.109

5.110

5.111

5.112

large sheets of stone or polished granite. These are often laid in a grid pattern, thus denying the building any load-bearing character, which stone facings laid in courses would have provided.

Brick-faced buildings often highlight the numerous instances where their building construction does not adequately reflect, and often totally ignores, any sense of structure [5.110]. To employ soldier arches is structurally illiterate, as they are incapable of carrying any load; but to avoid the expression, however nominal, of any lintel or arch, demeans not only the material, but the quality of the building itself. Even where a lintel has been introduced in the lower openings, it is not seen to be supported by the adjacent piers, as defined by contrasting brick. Such details, when viewed collectively, either make a convincing, structurally legible building, or create a wallpaper effect—a matter

often brought into sharp focus by comparison with older buildings.

In order for a building to be structurally honest and likely to harmonise with its surroundings, it should act as a clear diagram illustrating how the various parts of the building support each other. Where this is not shown, a visually unsatisfactory design will usually result [5.111]. Here the columns puncturing the sloping brick soffit create a most disconcerting result; they have no visible point of connection with the main body of the building, to which they are meant to lend support.

INTEGRITY OF INDIVIDUAL BUILDINGS

There is often pressure to increase a site area, to accommodate a scale of building and uses that cannot be contained within the framework of an

existing site. In certain situations, such an increase in scale and site area can be achieved successfully in townscape terms, by combining sites behind retained frontages, where existing floor levels and fenestration permit. Alternatively, one façade may be retained while a new building is erected on the adjoining site.

When, as in most cases, this results in a difference of architectural character between two seemingly individual buildings, it makes no sense to then provide an integrated roof treatment, perhaps running across several frontages. The object of preserving something of the grain of the area is defeated if, at the same time, the impression that the retained building is just a façade is unnecessarily reinforced [5.112].

When dealing with a terrace location, where the roof design may be unified, party walls, chimneys and other architectural features should be retained to provide the subdivision and

5.113

5.114

entrance, together with its prominent flight of steps, has been removed, interrupting the rhythm of the group.

Another form of linking at ground level is the introduction of a common fascia band, which produces a new frontage out of scale with the established pattern [5.114]. It is usually perfectly feasible to provide adequate visual association between one building and another, without resorting to a unifying architectural treatment. This is a particularly insensitive example in which the new central pilaster does not even coincide with the party wall. This kind of treatment is the result of marketing concepts which demand a high profile street presence. Yet unified identity can find even more extreme manifestations [5.115]. Here, not only have the ground floors been combined, but the upper floors as well, with a very distinctive treatment, to form one single unit. The retailers concerned have been giving an encouraging lead in re-establishing first-floor trading, and thereby helping to overcome a national problem of unused, unkempt upper floor accommodation in shopping areas. But given the decision to keep the façade of the corner building, it could have been adapted in a less drastic fashion so that the two upper brick storeys did not sit so awkwardly on the panelled walling system below.

BUILDING PROFILES

For far too long, the scenic and evocative potential of enriching our townscapes by using the profiles of buildings has been ignored. This is due partly to the influence of Modernist architecture, which banished all those delightful elements that in the past designers had exploited to the full. Hence the relentlessly stark outlines of so many twentieth-century buildings [5.116].

Historically, buildings were conceived partly to be seen against dramatic and constantly changing skies, so features such as chimneys, gables, dormers and turrets occurred in profusion. Buildings appeared to be in competition with each other to achieve the maximum visual impact— something which clients have always

interest created by such elements. They also express and enforce the individuality of each building within the whole composition. The unification of space behind the frontages of different buildings can be most disturbing at lower levels when viewed from the street. In order to overcome this problem, depending upon the fenestration it may be possible either to keep the existing compartments immediately behind the frontages, or at least to retain party walls for a certain depth from the front wall, thus

retaining some visual separation between building frontages in plan, as well as in elevation. Nothing looks worse than continuous bands of ceiling lighting running behind apparently different buildings.

When two or more sites are linked together, there is frequently a desire to extinguish one or other of the street entrances [5.113]. When a terrace is designed as a series of individual units forming part of a larger whole, features such as doorways are essential indications of separate identity. Here the

5.115

5.116

5.117

5.118

required; but this was accomplished at no cost to the general townscape.

The seemingly inescapable problem of leaking flat roofs apart, there are grounds for some optimism that more traditional roof forms are being employed by some designers, who are once again concerned to exploit the profiles of their buildings in a creative way [5.117]. All over the country, a second generation of shopping centre developments is being constructed. Unlike their rather dismal '60s counterparts, there appears to be a greater concern to break down their scale by the introduction of more fragmented rooflines and the creation of identity markers such as cupolas or bell towers.

The extent of conservation and rehabilitation work currently being carried out has serious implications for our skylines. Of course this process is vital to keep centres alive and conserve the building fabric; but the predictable pressure for additional space, which frequently involves radical changes at roof level, should be resisted where a distinctive profile would be compromised [5.118]. In this unique and well-known example, the ability to see the cinquefoil balustrade silhouetted against the sky has been lost, particularly in longer views across the adjacent open space.

Buildings will frequently present different profiles depending upon the viewpoint. The roof may be read as part of the wider skyline in urban spaces such as a square, or where they close a view down a street. In these situations the roof may be seen in full elevation [5.119]. In a typical market square, the mixture of building styles and heights produces a varied skyline. On closer examination, the second building from the right has been rebuilt and has lost something during the process. Exceptionally narrow plot widths are particularly characteristic of this space. A relatively successful attempt has been made to convey an impression that there are still two buildings on the site. But the overscaled and unified roof treatment cuts across this apparent subdivision. The lack of party walls and chimneys lends this roof a stark appearance—a loss hardly compensated for by the unsightly plant room.

5.119

5.120

Perhaps a more common situation is where the profile is formed by the parapet or eaves seen obliquely from the street below [5.120]. Dormer windows are a traditional way of interrupting the skyline. These three dormers, together with the crested ridge tiles, enliven an otherwise plain pitched roof. The decorative trefoil window arches are echoed by the curved bargeboards to the dormers. They establish a visual link between the architecture of the street façade and the profile of the building.

5.121

bulary, this separation has become blurred. In certain cases, as a response to daylight angles and other massing constraints, designers have produced tier upon tier of set-backs treated identically to the main frontage. Far from breaking down the scale, this approach tends, if anything, to increase the apparent size of a development. Alternatively, they resort to what has mockingly been termed 'planner's mansard', with some awkward results [5.121]. In this largely nineteenth-century planned area where the roofs are underplayed, the introduction of the double-decker mansard appears particularly baffling. Given the prominent corner site, and the scale and height of the neighbouring buildings, the façade could have been carried up by at least another

Roofscapes

The roofscapes of our towns and cities have seriously deteriorated during the last thirty years or so. This has been caused by a number of factors. The proliferation of lift motor rooms and mechanical plant has tended to spoil new and refurbished buildings alike. Modern roofscapes are characterised by large, flat areas covered in bitumen or gravel, only interrupted by guard rails, defining escape routes, or the tracks for window cleaning equipment.

The pervasive argument that what goes up on the roof will never be seen, at least not from ground level, tends to encourage an attitude which discounts the potentially creative use of roofs, not only visually but also for recreational purposes. The fact that for many office workers or inner-city residents views of the resulting sterile and ugly wasteland are their only outlook is given barely a second thought.

The dramatic increase in the scale of development sites has meant that roofscapes can often become oversized and too prominent, especially since the welcome return of the 'pitched roof'. Traditionally the distinction between street façade and roof has been clearly drawn. Indeed, during the eighteenth and much of the nineteenth centuries, roofs were deliberately understated, or designed out altogether. In the absence of an established architectural voca-

5.122

floor, which would have avoided the top-heavy effect.

The last decade or so has witnessed some bizarre attempts to disguise overdevelopment by experimenting with roof forms. They have also been employed to provide new developments with greater individuality and visual presence, with the result that roofs have tended to become more prominent [5.122]. Visually overwhelming, the effect created by this roof is exaggerated by the deep shadows and lack of any subdivision, apart from the close rhythm of joints in the metal cladding. Again, the roofscape appears quite out of proportion, as if it belonged to a much larger building beyond, or had been temporarily roofed over during repairs.

The size of roofs can be difficult to handle at a smaller scale, particularly on exposed or sloping sites [5.123]. The roof here has been broken down by the stepped massing, which creates a complex form that responds to the steeply sloping site, while not detracting from the prominence enjoyed by the church spire beyond.

5.123

Even on level ground, roofscapes can assume visual importance [5.124]. The gable, set backs, dormers and chimneys of this housing development sited on a gentle curve produce the right degree of interest and complexity. The resulting roofscape harmonizes well with its neighbour.

5.124

Plant

Rapid developments in micro-technology and the resulting wide-spread use of computers, VDUs and associated air-conditioning in a variety of buildings have led to an ever-increasing demand for space to house the mechanical plant required. In addition, many organisations are insisting on stand-by generators to safeguard against interruptions in the supply of electrical power. While a significant percentage of this equipment can be housed underground, there will inevitably be some plant that will always need to be accommodated at roof level.

Changes in legislation aimed at achieving greater safety at work, particularly related to maintenance access, have also built in spatial requirements that have led to an increase in the overall size and bulk of plant enclosures.

It is not always easy to predict the likely demands for future expansion, or anticipate changes in working practices and technological innovations. The provision for such facilities appears regularly to be underestimated, especially in speculative developments—perhaps to gain a speedy planning approval, or to achieve the maximum floorspace. Subsequently, planning authorities are frequently requested to approve additional plant, sometimes even before the scheme concerned is completed. While this situation continues, it will be virtually impossible to provide satisfactory roofscapes.

Planning authorities should encourage designers always to provide scope for expansion of mechanical plant in schemes put forward for formal approval. Carefully considered and agreed roof designs achieved at the planning stage can then be retained intact, at least for a reasonable period into the future.

When considering the location of plant accommodation, it can be advantageous to set the plant well back from the building frontage, where the site depth and position of the core allow [5.125]. But, as this example demonstrates, it can still be visually dominant when viewed from street level.

5.125

5.126

Usually the siting of the core on plan will be critical. Obviously, the means of escape travel distances are just one of many, often conflicting, requirements that influence the internal layout. Service cores inevitably run the full height of the building, plus associated lift motor rooms. Their likely impact on the roofscape and surrounding skylines will need to be assessed at an early stage in the design process. There may be scope to make a visual feature of these elements, but in many instances, due to their size, their unacceptable appearance on the roofline may dictate an alternative location for the core. To an important extent, designers can be the victims, willing or otherwise, of their own self-deception. Certainly, at planning submission stage, plant rooms are hardly ever shown realistically on presentation drawings. If they do appear at all, they are indicated in the thinnest of lines, almost to the point of being transparent. But in the cold light of day they are transformed into very solid, hard-edged boxes.

Plant on a newly completed building can all too frequently assume an importance which was never intended, by being seen above the roofs of other buildings. This detracts not only from their appearance, but also from the overall visual quality and character of the surrounding area [5.126]. As in this instance, sites in the vicinity of open spaces, such as squares, require particular vigilance because longer views of their plant can be obtained.

A particular characteristic of so many of our urban centres is their irregular street pattern. This often provides full views of buildings, especially where the street changes direction [5.127], such as on this gentle curve. The rounded profile of the attic storey, which forms the building's skyline in closer views, has been carefully considered as an integral part of the design. It is unfortunate, therefore, that the plant located above this level appears, in longer views, as an unrelated afterthought, upsetting the overall composition.

The importance of chimneys and their architectural potential has traditionally been recognised and exploited to the full. Now that they are no longer needed, new opportunities to create

5.127

intricate skylines are presented by the need to accommodate the ever-increasing amounts of mechanical plant at roof level [5.128]. This is an all too rare example of what can be achieved with a little imagination. Louvred ventilation ducts take the form of chimneys and dormers, and have been arranged to produce a dramatic roofscape entirely in character with the surroundings.

The installation of a lift when buildings are being converted can often be problematic [5.129]. This convinc-

ing attempt to disguise a liftshaft complete with full classical detailing is, nonetheless, out of scale and dominates the building it serves. A less formalised treatment would have been more successful.

5.128

5.129

MATERIALS: SELECTION AND USE

The governing principle, when initially considering the selection of materials to be used in a specific location, is respect for the established or indigenous materials to be found in the area. In recent years, there has been an almost perverse instinct on the part of many architects to introduce new and alien facing materials all over the country. The supposed universality and arrogance of the International Style—no respecter of national, let alone regional or local characteristics, or of cultural identity—played an important role in creating this anarchic climate. The insidious influence of the concept of corporate identity has also driven multiple retailers to stamp a standardised image across the country, irrespective of the local context.

Yet another powerful reason for parting company with the materials of the surrounding area, especially for speculative developments, is to produce visual impact in the street. And one of the easiest ways to create such an impression is to introduce a drastically different material, reinforced by an alien colour and finish [5.130]. Here dark grey glass has been used in what is almost exclusively a granite and stone area.

In the past there was a discernible hierarchy of building materials associated not only with particular building types, but also with different classes within each type. This provided visual clues to the relative status of particular parts of the townscape, and allowed these areas to have an identity of their own. For instance, brick generally came at the bottom of the scale, with stone and other natural materials regarded as being most prestigious. In between these came brick with simple stone or stucco embellishments, and, further up the scale, stucco, terracotta and faience. The selection of materials today should equally respond to this and the designer should be aware of the possibility of employing a range of materials. A hierarchy also operated within an individual site. The principal façade would be faced in Portland stone, while secondary frontages

might be finished in stucco or brick, and the detailing was often reduced in richness. This helped to maintain a legible distinction between principal and secondary streets, a feature denied in so many current schemes, where there is a distinct trend to adopt a solution and continue it right around the site. The scale of the development is then exaggerated, which is in direct conflict with making good townscape.

Combination

There are numerous examples where different facing materials have been combined to produce an interesting effect, adding greatly to the visual interest and quality of a building. Such a contrast can be introduced to highlight particular features by combining different varieties of the same material, such as stock brickwork with contrasting red-rubbers for window arches, or, alternatively, a juxtaposition of quite different materials, like brick and faience [5.131]. The Victorians frequently used straightforward brickwork with richly detailed faience or terracotta. In this modern example, plain brickwork has been combined with unrelieved flat blocks of faience for the spandrels. These seem to cry out for some form of decoration, and the end product appears impoverished.

A noticeable feature of recent brick-faced developments is the lack of any contrast between materials [5.132]. The use of one material, often a vibrant red brick without stone or stucco to lighten the design, can create a lumpen and monotonous effect.

Texture, colour and tone

Another trend has been for materials to become more sombre. Designers have tended to use a deeper palette: dark, often unrelieved brickwork, and matching mortar, are teamed with dark tinted glass in bronze-finished frames, combined with a darker range of polished granites [5.133]. The overall impression is made even more oppressive by our often overcast skies. For weathering reasons, the tradition has evolved of the use of polished granite at ground level. But this finish

5.130

5.131

5.132

used in larger areas, as in this example, introduces specular reflection to such an extent that, when viewed obliquely, it is impossible to differentiate between polished granite and glass. Polishing, incidentally, is the most expensive finish. It inevitably makes the granite appear much darker than other finishes and is generally less compatible with established townscapes.

When selecting materials, it may not be wise to match the apparent tone or colour of adjacent buildings precisely. They may have weathered and be subject to cleaning, radically altering the character of whole areas. It is, however, always important to respect the tonal range in any location. Designers have not been timid in their use of colour in the past. It appears that today we suffer from the tyranny of cream and black for our early nineteenth-century stuccoed terraces when originally they were decorated in far less restrained schemes. There are indications that designers are again learning to experiment with colour, particularly with the use of a range of materials and colourful powder-coated window frames.

5.133

5.134

Local variations

In different regions, certain localised uses of materials have become part of the established vernacular. This can also be related to local adaptations of national styles and constructional details, all of which contribute to creating a sense of place [5.134]. The drip mould above the window, an essentially Gothic feature, is combined with an otherwise classically inspired version of Welsh Georgian.

Wherever a local tradition exists concerning the use of specific building materials, it should be reflected in new developments. Clearly, employing local materials will not by itself result in making good townscape, but their appropriate use will be a vital step in that direction. The selection of a particular local material and its inherent characteristics should, if used seriously, tend to suggest a design more likely to harmonise with the surrounding character.

Detailing

A notable failing in recent building is the lack of detailing and, where it does occur, its often rudimentary nature [5.135]. It is this aspect, perhaps more than any other, that distinguishes recent architecture from its earlier counterparts. The welcome return to more traditional forms of expression only serves to highlight the problem. Expectations have been raised, now that careful stitching together appears to be the order of the day; new buildings are expected to compete with their predecessors on equal terms, and are judged accordingly.

There are some major obstacles today which designers in the past did not have to contend with, including the myriad requirements controlling building construction. Now that the majority of urban buildings have a framed structure, their external faces are simply applied and non-load-bearing. Clearly this has a crucial influence on the detailed design. One of the most obvious factors is the inclusion of mastic-filled compression joints that run horizontally and vertically across the face of the building. It is possible to avoid these becoming too apparent by tucking them under string courses, or in the reveal of projecting piers.

The scale at which details are considered is equally crucial. At 1:50 scale, drawings can appear cluttered and designs over-fussy; whereas, at full size, the same detail would seem stark and simplistic, particularly in a historic context. This is a common shortcoming, due in large measure to a lack of experience, not only in the quality of detail, but also in gauging the apparent scale and projection of details when viewed from the ground. It is a skill that can be acquired only by trial and error, together with thoughtful appreciation of built examples.

Traditionally, brickwork has been exploited for its pattern-making potential, as well as the opportunities it presents for creating architectural forms. Several recent designs have attempted to produce a similar effect [5.136]. Here the pattern is quite decorative, but its mosaic-like quality does not convey the character of a load-bearing wall—a point reinforced by the soldier arches over the windows. For all its inventiveness, the two-

5.136

5.135

dimensional character creates an impression of meanness and superficiality.

However, there are current examples where brickwork has been so well detailed that it stands comparison with Victorian and Edwardian work [5.137]. Bay windows are frequently incorporated into a design to provide modelling, and often tend to overwhelm the overall concept. Rarely are they introduced with such subtlety. Note the care with which the soffit of the lower bay has been nicely finished off. However, a comparison with its neighbour, which the onlooker is almost invited to make, does highlight the relative flatness of the new façade. It lacks the vigorous cornices that would have assisted in counterbalancing the visual weight of the bays. This failing has also resulted in unsightly streaking at the bottom of the picture, which a projecting cornice could have helped to control.

When employing historically familiar elements, without plenty of experience or a good eye it can be difficult to achieve the right balance between individual parts. Frequently, cornices are hopelessly underscaled, while other features can be crude and out of proportion with the design as a whole [5.138]. The console brackets on the left are of a gargantuan scale, dwarfing the adjacent brick piers, with crude pads acting as capitals of some sort. A

5.137

5.138

5.139

point that is often overlooked is that in urban areas, particularly in commercial streets, brickwork was not often used below first-floor level—this being treated in stone or stucco. Its use here tends to fragment the overall design and create a discordant effect.

A paper thin, transitory quality seems to be the hallmark of so much recent building. As already discussed, this is partly the result of constructional techniques; but even within such constraints it is possible to avoid the impression of veneering [5.139]. The lively interplay of different surfaces produced on a conventional framed structure is a demonstration of the potential to create expressive detailing.

Traditionally many of the buildings in our urban centres were visually connected and were seen almost to embrace each other with overlapping cornices and mouldings. The junctions between new and existing buildings, however, tend to be problematic: site measurements do not necessarily correspond with surveys, and gaps can occur which are difficult to detail satisfactorily. This is a situation that can detract from both buildings, but one which can be overcome if given enough thought at an early stage in the design development. Some flexibility will need to be built in so that junction details can accommodate the inevitable tolerances.

A common method for overcoming or side-stepping this problem has been the widespread use of the flash gap, which involves the formation of a re-entrant, where the two frontages do not come into direct visual contact. It was a particularly popular device with Modern architects, who attempted thus to create a neutral buffer zone between disparate architectures [5.140]. As in this case, escape stairs or service entrances were frequently placed next to party walls, and treated in a so-called 'neutral' manner. A major objection to this practice is that it leads to the visual fragmentation of familiar corridor streets, formed as they are by tightly packed, sometimes overlapping frontages. In other cases vestigial party walls can obstruct a clean juxtaposition. Now that designers are experimenting with histori-

5.140

5.141

cal elements such as cornices, junctions and party wall agreements are of more direct interest to them.

Weathering

The selection of the basic facing material of any building, particularly in our climate, will be of vital importance to its long-term appearance. Over the last thirty years or so, traditional materials such as stone and granite have continued to be used, but detailed in a non-traditional way, mainly as a facing material in thin sheets. Architectural features that facilitated their natural weathering qualities, such as projecting cornices, drip moulds and sills, have been absent. This has resulted in unsightly staining and different weathering [5.141] While

5.142

5.143

this example has some modelling, and horizontal blocking courses, these have not been appropriately detailed and staining has resulted.

Splayed sills and soffits have been a particularly prevalent design feature during the last few decades [5.142], but they encourage unsightly streaking that detracts from the prestige of the building concerned. In sweeping away what was generally regarded by the Modern Movement as heretical, non-functional ornament, architects have actually encouraged Mother Nature to do her worst. In fact, well-considered detailing should control weathering to add to, rather than detract from, the visual quality of our built environment and reduce maintenance costs.

Decorative potential

Decoration can be a very emotive topic for discussion in architectural circles. During the three centuries which preceded our own, a classical vocabulary had developed, with each period providing a particular interpretation of the general theme. This came to an abrupt halt when Modernism gained supremacy and ornament and decoration were effectively banished for being non-functional. In fact they had played a central role, particularly in the nineteenth century, in explaining and promoting the role and status of a building's occupiers; sculptural groups, for instance, illustrated aspects of trade and commerce [5.143]. The dramatic contrast between these two buildings, both designed to serve a banking function, demonstrates the visual bankruptcy of so much recent architecture.

Decoration has been censored for so long that whole generations of designers are unfamiliar with its use and have become accustomed to an aesthetic straitjacket. Standardisation and industrialised building techniques have led to a reduction in the range of interesting details. An ever-diminishing percentage of building costs is spent on the external face of the design, while there has been a very significant increase, in percentage terms, in the sums spent on services.

More encouragingly, there is a genuine search on the part of many designers to discover, or rediscover, forms to enrich their buildings and provide meaning and a relevant iconography for the present day. Figurative sculpture has always performed an important role in architectural expression, and is beginning to return [5.144]. The bas-relief female busts in the metal frieze represent an early and not altogether successful return towards sculpture. They fail to provide the required visual stop to the façade, or to the visual delight of the elegant paired putti supporting swags in the adjacent classical entablature.

Wherever possible, it is desirable for most sculptural elements to be formed of the same base material as the body of the building [5.145]. Here, allegorical granite figures are set within an architectural framework and are very much part of the overall design.

By using terracotta or faience it is possible to produce quite complex detailing, and decorative patterns, with relative ease [5.146]. This Victorian example combines terracotta with brickwork and granite. The former is a much neglected material, and is especially applicable to locations surrounded by architecture with a rich surface texture. The decorative potential of natural materials can be enhanced by exploiting their inherent characteristics; with granite, for instance, different surface treatments such as fine-axed, honed or flame textured can significantly alter its appearance.

Brick continues to be the most widespread of all building materials. In the nineteenth century, particularly for Victorian industrial and commercial architecture, brickwork was employed to interpret an architectural language which in grander buildings would have been executed in stone or stucco. Designers have much greater

5.144

5.145

5.146

5.147

5.148

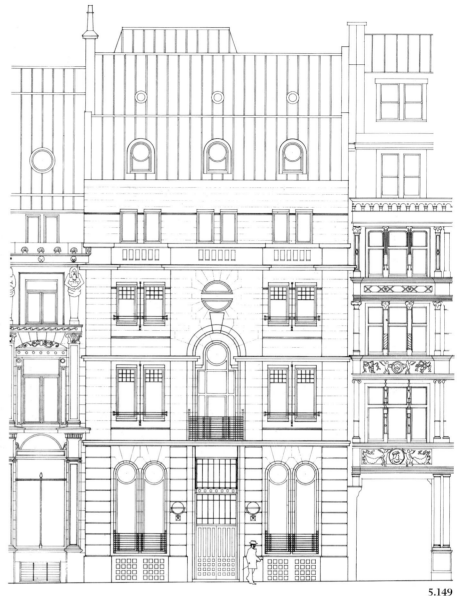

5.149

freedom to introduce decoration now that an increasing number of brick specials are becoming available [5.147]. In this recent example, a convincing system of articulation has been produced. It is regrettable that thoughtful detailing of this quality is the exception rather than the rule. It appears that few brick-faced commercial buildings of recent years have any pretensions towards architecture.

There has also been a long tradition the use of metalwork for its decorative potential. This has taken the form of roof cresting, balconies, grilles, rain water goods and door furniture. These elements provide an additional layer of decoration which, although small in scale, can register in the townscape [5.148]. In this example, the cast-iron columns, cornice and other features assume the importance of primary architectural elements. The modern use of cast-iron can easily replicate past designs and produce exciting new ones.

DESIGN ILLUSTRATION

The way in which designs are illustrated and presented is of considerable importance, yet judging by the general standard of presentation, this is not always appreciated. For instance, it is not uncommon for drawings still to be submitted for planning permission which do not show adjoining buildings. A design drawn in isolation will often have been conceived in isolation.

Drawings continue to be an indespensable medium to express ideas. Historically, buildings have been presented in plan, section and elevation [5.149]. Today these drawings still form the basic means of communication. Other methods are, how-ever, being introduced, and some of the larger architectural practices now have computers which can plot building heights and outlines and project them into a given view. While the resulting print-outs do have limitations in conveying the character and detail of a design, there is no doubt that computers are likely to play an increasingly important role. At the same time it must be said that at present only a small percentage of designers have ready access to these advanced pieces of office equipment.

5.150

5.151

Perspective drawings

There is a long tradition in the use of the art of perspective. The great nineteenth-century competition drawings demonstrate the considerable efforts made to provide a realistic, if somewhat heroic, impression. Perspectives can provide a convincing way of illustrating a scheme [5.150]. This example allows minimum scope for misrepresentation, as can be judged by comparing it with a photograph of the completed building [5.151].

In other situations, where the bulk and height of a scheme or its potential impact on local views may be critical, the use of perspectives will not be appropriate. The simple fact is that such drawings cannot be relied upon and not infrequently illustrate views which cannot be enjoyed. Another serious drawback is that if the existing context of a new building is rendered in the same technique as the new design, this will inevitably make it appear more appropriate and 'at home' than actually would be the case.

In these drawings, existing buildings are usually greatly simplified, whereas new designs are shown in full, glowing detail. In the absence of recognisable fixed points there is bound to be scope, however inadvertent, for inaccuracies, adjustments, and sadly, on occasion, deception.

Currently there is a vogue in architectural perspective for the 'economical' line drawing. As artwork these drawings can be very attractive [5.152]. But they do not, in the absence of other information, provide a realistic impression or form the basis upon which a full townscape assessment can be made. Here, both buildings in the foreground are new and their architectural detail is not complex. A particular shortcoming of this graphic style is that it gives no sense of materials or surface texture. In fact the buildings were constructed in brick and reconstituted stone, as can be seen from the photograph of the completed scheme taken from approximately the same position as the perspective [5.153].

5.152

5.153

The photomontage

An increasingly familiar method of illustrating buildings, the photo-montage has the great advantage of providing planners, clients and members of the public, who may be unfamiliar with the abstractions of elevations, and isometrics taken from strange angles, with as realistic an impression as possible of the design *in situ* [5.154]. It is interesting to compare this montage with the building as constructed.

Several montages may be required of one scheme, depending upon the complexities of the site. Viewpoints should be agreed with local planners in advance. The quality of the original photograph is crucial. It is probably best to use a 4 in (127 × 101 mm) plate camera in order to avoid any distortion. This technique requires that the position, height and focal length of the camera be known, from which a basic line drawing can then be calculated. In order to avoid costly and abortive artwork, it may be useful to try and establish the basic bulk and massing criteria prior to producing the finished artwork ready for montaging. This should appear to be more like a photograph than a line drawing using

5.154

5.155

5.156

5.157

tones. Attention should be paid to casting shadows and the way architectural features and materials are portrayed to create an effective result.

Architectural models

Models have been used for centuries to illustrate architectural concepts, and a small but thriving industry continues to produce these seductively crafted objects. Their particular appeal is possibly due, in part, to the role of 'creator' they offer to the onlooker. Models used as a design tool seem to be rare, although they have great potential, especially for considering and illustrating roofscapes, which montages or perspectives taken from street level fail to cover adequately.

Instead, models of the highly finished variety, their surrounding streets trafficked by models of the most expensive motor cars, tend to appear solely for the benefit of planning or board meetings. The problem is that they frequently materialise late in the day, partly because of the time required for their manufacture. Thus, in spite of the shortcomings which they often highlight, there is an understandable reluctance to have them changed.

It is also possible to use models, providing the scale and detail is adequate, for photomontages [5.156]. Instead of using artwork, a photograph of a model can be montaged to produce a reasonably convincing result for very little additional cost. It is instructive to compare the resulting montage with a line drawing of the same design, taken from a different viewpoint [5.157].

When deciding how to illustrate a design, the overall aim should be to give as fair a representation as possible of the proposal to those who are funding it, to those responsible for giving it planning permission and, perhaps above all, to the local community who will have to live with the end-product.

Conclusion

Our intention in writing this book has been to provide encouragement and positive guidance for all those involved, directly and indirectly, in the realisation of buildings in an urban context. We are greatly encouraged by the widespread conclusion, shared by many professionals and interested laypeople, that the restrictive 'no alternative' tenets of the Modern Movement have failed dismally to create a satisfactory environment. As a result, many designers are attempting to pick up the threads of an earlier townscape and architectural tradition.

There is, however, a distinct danger of this process descending into a form of 'decorated Modernism', where superficial decorative motifs are served up and applied in a haphazard fashion, without the required understanding of their real purpose. While these schemes may be ostensibly more attractive than their predecessors, it is highly questionable as to whether they represent a real advance. But in spite of this serious reservation, the underlying trend clearly amounts to something more than a temporary, eclectic nostalgia trip. It reflects a genuine desire to establish once again a living tradition of crafting good

buildings which are seen to form a natural part of their surroundings.

The fact that such a tradition has been absent for so long means that this task is considerable and may take several generations to achieve. There is no longer a mode of thought that automatically takes context into account. In attempting to set out the framework of a contextual approach and method of design, it is therefore necessary to start from basic principles.

The town itself should be the first consideration, its size, geographical setting and its *raison d'être*, past and present, so that the designer can gain an overall sense of the kind of town his project is destined for and how the two are likely to interact. The wider context having been established, the specific characteristics of the site itself can be better studied and understood. Too often in the past this process has been a myopic exercise restricted to the site boundary. The contextualist approach, on the other hand, takes into account the townscape role of the site, the existing buildings, and identifies what should be expected of new buildings in relating to adjoining ones.

Although we have not set out specifically to promote conservation,

this book aims to be complementary to the legislative framework and the philosophy it embodies, which the conservation movement fought so hard to secure.

Before a detailed evaluation of the site and its context leads to the formulation of a sketch design, there is one central aspect which has to be dealt with, and that is the client's brief. His requirements should be tested against the site and local planning policies to identify potential conflicts, for example over density or use. Good townscape can only result when the requirements of the brief and the site can be satisfactorily resolved. The act of weaving together should stem naturally from a knowledge of the site, its immediate surroundings and the wider setting. By responding to these, the designer should find a source of inspiration which transcends any preconceived ideas. Far from creating a straitjacket, this essentially pragmatic approach should set up a creative interaction which can but benefit the resulting design, and thereby assist positively in making townscapes of enduring quality.

Selected reading list

(in order of publication)

Books

SITTE, CAMILLO, *City Planning according to Artistic Principles*, Vienna, 1889. Republished in English by Phaidon Press, 1965

EDWARDS, TRYSTAN, *Good and Bad Manners in Architecture*, Philip Allan, 1924

JOHNS, EWART, *Townscape*, 1958

GIBBERD, FREDERICK, *Town Design*, Architectural Press, 1959

MINISTRY OF HOUSING AND LOCAL GOVERNMENT, *Historic Towns. Preservation and Change*, HMSO, 1967

SHARP, THOMAS, *Town and Townscape*, John Murray, 1968

WORSKETT, ROY, *The Character of Towns: An approach to Conservation*, Architectural Press, 1969

CULLEN, GORDON, *The Concise Townscape*, Architectural Press, paperback reprint, 1971

SMITH, PETER F., *The Dynamics of Urbanism*, Hutchinson Educational, 1974

BURKE, GERALD, *Townscapes*, Pelican, 1976

BROLIN, BRENT C., *Architecture in Context: Fitting new buildings with old*, New York, Van Nostrand Reinhold, 1980

BENTLEY, IAN, *et al.*, *Responsive Environments*, Architectural Press, 1985

Journals (special issues cited in the text)

NAIRN, IAN (ed.), 'Outrage', *The Architectural Review*, June, 1955

NAIRN, IAN (ed.), 'Counter Attack', *The Architectural Review*, December, 1956

DE WOLFE, IVOR (ed.), 'SLOAP', *The Architectural Review*, October, 1973

Index